THE TRAVELS OF RICHARD TRAUNTER

EARLY AMERICAN HISTORIES

Douglas Bradburn, John C. Coombs, and S. Max Edelson, Editors

THE TRAVELS OF RICHARD TRAUNTER

Two Journeys through the Native Southeast in 1698 and 1699

Edited by Sandra L. Dahlberg

University of Virginia Press
Charlottesville and London

University of Virginia Press
© 2022 by the Rector and Visitors of the University of Virginia
All rights reserved
Printed in the United States of America on acid-free paper

First published 2022

1 3 5 7 9 8 6 4 2

Library of Congress Cataloging-in-Publication Data

Names: Traunter, Richard, author. | Dahlberg, Sandra L., editor.
Title: The travels of Richard Traunter : two journeys through the native southeast in 1698 and 1699 / edited by Sandra L. Dahlberg.
Other titles: Early American histories.
Description: Charlottesville : University of Virginia Press, 2022. | Series: Early American histories | Includes bibliographical references and index.
Identifiers: LCCN 2022026789 (print) | LCCN 2022026790 (ebook) | ISBN 9780813947785 (hardcover ; alkaline paper) | ISBN 9780813947792 (paperback) | ISBN 9780813947808 (ebook)
Subjects: LCSH: Traunter, Richard—Travel—Virginia. | Traunter, Richard—Travel—North Carolina. | Traunter, Richard—Travel—South Carolina. | Indians of North America—Virginia—Social life and customs—17th century. | Indians of North America—North Carolina—Social life and customs—17th century. | Indians of North America—South Carolina—Social life and customs—17th century. | White people—Relations with Indians—History. | LCGFT: Diaries. | Travel writing.
Classification LCC F212 .T73 2022 (print) | LCC F212 (ebook) | DDC 305.897/075—dc23/eng/20220623
LC record available at https://lccn.loc.gov/2022026789
LC ebook record available at https://lccn.loc.gov/2022026790

Cover art: Detail of *Map of the several nations of Indians to the Northwest of South Carolina,* Francis Nicholson. (Library of Congress, Geography and Map Division, G3860 1724 .M2 1929)

Contents

Acknowledgments vii

Editorial Method ix

Introduction xi

THE TRAVELS OF RICHARD TRAUNTER 1

The Preface 7

Journal One—1698: A Journal of my Travels from Appopmatox River in Virginia, to Charles Town in South Carolina by Land 11

Journal Two—1699: An Exact Journal of my Second Voyage from Virginia to South Carolina by Land Anno 1699 35

Appendix A. The Humble Memorial of Edward Loughton and Richard Tranter 57

Appendix B. The Humble Memorial of John Smith 61

Appendix C. An Abstract of the Proceedings Relating to the Discovery of Silver Mines in Carolina 65

Appendix D. Jean Couture, Letter to the English Board of Trade 67

Bibliography 69

Index 87

Acknowledgments

I want to thank all the individuals and institutions who supported my research for this book. The University of Houston–Downtown and its English Department provided resources that enabled me to conduct the necessary archival research in Virginia and in the United Kingdom. I am appreciative of the archivists and staff at the Virginia Museum of History and Culture who facilitated my visits to their archive, especially Frances Pollard and John McClure, as well as Matthew Guillen and Andrew Foster, who were quickly responsive to email inquiries. Thanks go to Zoe Stansell at the British Library for tracking down the auction details for Traunter's manuscript. I am grateful for the observations of Alexander Moore, Alan Briceland, and Vera Keller that guided my initial investigations. I am also deeply indebted to James H. Merrell, whose generous feedback on the book drafts was invaluable. Most especially, my warm thanks go to Nadine Zimmerli at the University of Virginia Press for her support and encouragement throughout this process. Finally, I am grateful for Peter Greenfield's steady reassurance and his patience when I worked out loud as this book took shape.

Editorial Method

This edition of *The Travels of Richard Traunter* maintains most of its seventeenth-century characteristics to preserve the quality of Traunter's voice. Traunter's original spelling, abbreviated words, and punctuation (or lack thereof) have been retained. Interlineations have been silently incorporated into the text as have Traunter's deletions and corrections. Italics denote Traunter's use of display script. For reading ease, the formatting of Traunter's journal dates has been standardized with full calendric detail added in brackets. Pagination for the original manuscript is provided in brackets marking the beginning of each page. A bracketed [P] marks the insertion of a paragraph break not in the original manuscript but added for reading clarity.

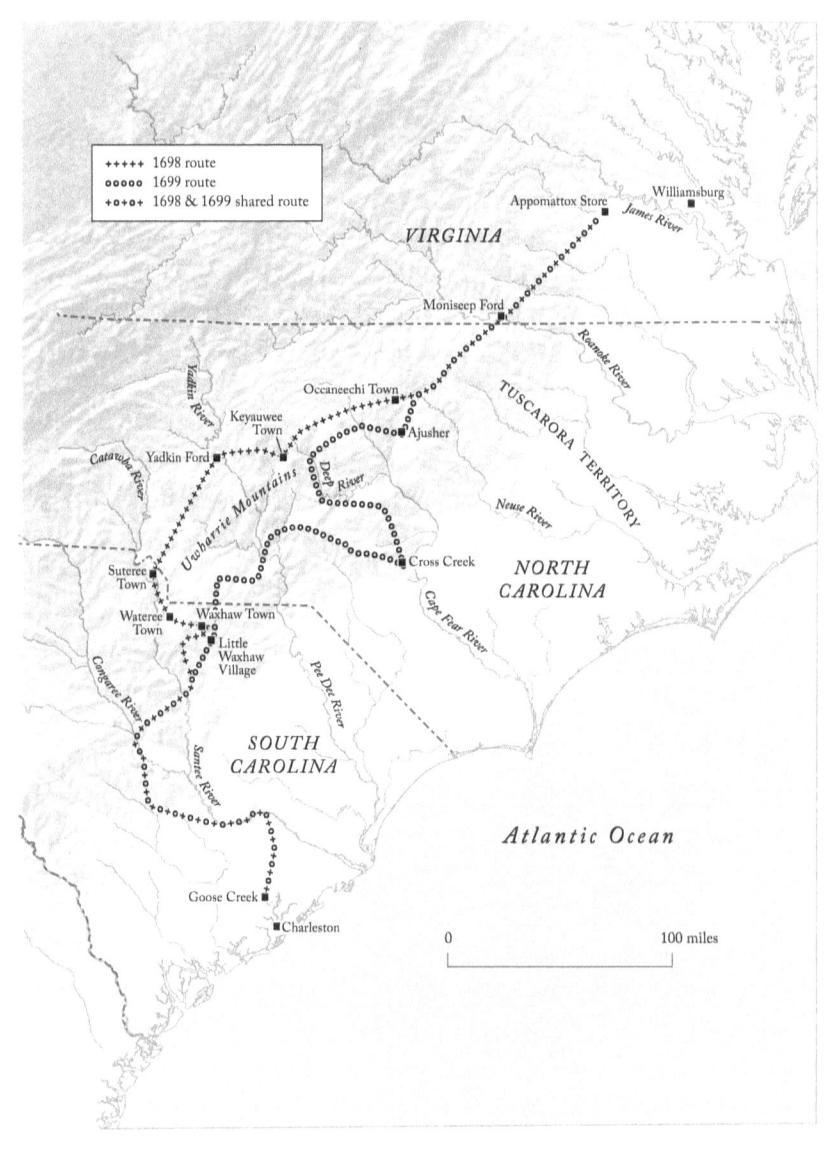

Map 1. Traunter's routes. (Nate Case, INCase, LLC)

Introduction

On the morning of 15 August 1698, a Virginia trader named Richard Traunter saddled his horse and set out from the trade store he managed on Appomattox River, headed for Charleston, South Carolina. He did not go alone. Eleven men, several dogs, and perhaps as many as a hundred horses went with him. Four of the men were traders who worked for Col. William Byrd, as did Traunter. An extensive trade business with Indians in the Southeast had made Byrd a wealthy man with considerable political clout in Virginia. Byrd supplied Traunter and his men with "good horses, Arms, Amunition, and provision" for their venture. This was not Traunter's first journey. He was an experienced trader and traveler who spoke no less than three Indigenous languages—Tuscarora, Wateree, and Waxhaw—attesting to many years of close contact with peoples south of Virginia. He and his party left Appomattox River as he had many times before, moving south on the "Virginia Traders path from one Indian Town to another."* Along the way they visited the Indian towns of Occaneechi, Keyauwee, Suteree, Wateree, and Waxhaw—as well as what may have been Congaree and Santee communities. The following September, in 1699, Traunter set out once again to scout a course through modern North Carolina that ran east of the Uwharrie Mountains. Only four men accompanied him this time, in addition to dogs and thirty-six horses.

At the time Traunter made his journeys, Native communities in the Southeast were experiencing unprecedented demographic dislocation. Siouan-

---

* The trade road was often identified by the Indian towns along its southward route: the Occaneechi Path, the Esaw or Catawba Path, and the Waxhaw Road, depending on the section. The number of horses estimated for 1698 was based on the ratio of horses to men Traunter had in 1699 when he traveled with four men and thirty-six horses. Traunter's logs are identified hereafter as Journal One (1698) and Journal Two (1699). See *The Travels of Richard Traunter*, preface, 10, and Journal Two, 36; see also Rights, "Trading Path to the Indians"; Dobbs, "Frontier Settlement Development."

INTRODUCTION

Iroquoian warfare caused some displacement, including the abandonment of an Eno town Traunter passed by. However, historian Paul Kelton and archaeologist Robin Beck have demonstrated that colonists' commerce in Indian slaves, combined with a smallpox epidemic, caused the greatest devastation. In the Suteree and Waxhaw towns, Traunter described the steadfast exertions of "Indian Doctors" to treat sickened people, yet few "escaped this Distemper" alive.* His observations of the Native Southeast were recorded in day-by-day logbooks for each trip that also enumerated the several species of plants, animals, fish, and fowl found in the region. At Moniseep Ford on the Roanoke River, for instance, Traunter wrote of "very Spacious Savanaes or Meadows intermix'd in divers places with most pleasant Groves . . . abounding with such variety of medicinall herbs" that it could be Aesculapius's garden. Road conditions were logged to show where rain-saturated water levels impeded passage, to mark the rocky terrains that were dangerous for horses, and to note fords where people and goods could be transported safely across waterways. His daily diet, mostly turkey, was catalogued along with directions on how to barbecue larger game. The journals were also a vehicle for Traunter's self-aggrandizement. Despite his claims that he persevered "in defiance of all danger from the Indians," an irate bear was the only danger Traunter faced. Traunter also portrayed himself as a diplomat who made peace with eight Indigenous nations with a commission given to Eno Will, Ajusher's headman, by which Indians pledged to "be kind to the Traders, and Suffer Carolina Men to come that way to Virginia and the Virginians to travell safe to Carolina." Englishmen transiting in the piedmont were rarely molested, but readers in England would not have known that.†

---

* Kelton, *Epidemics and Enslavement*, xviii, 147; Beck, *Chiefdoms, Collapse*, 15, 117, 124; Traunter, *Travels*, Journal One, 26–27. (The page numbers cited for Traunter's journals and appendices refer to this edition. Traunter's original manuscript pagination is shown in brackets to indicate the start of each handwritten page.) Changes to the human landscape can be discerned, as well, by comparing Traunter's account to those of previous travelers. Traunter encountered only one Indigenous site along the Virginia portion of the road at Monk's Neck Creek, a place Edward Bland identified as "the old fields of Manks Nessoneicks," already abandoned in 1650. Between Fort Henry and Roanoke River, Bland cited two Nottoway towns, a Meherrin town, and a Tuscarora town (*Discovery of New Brittaine*, 30, 130, 115–24).

† Traunter, *Travels*, Journal One, 16, 23, and preface, 10; Byrd II, "History of the Dividing Line," in *Prose Works*, 230; Davis, "Cultural Landscape of the North Carolina Piedmont," 152.

INTRODUCTION

We know all of this, and more besides, because amid the baggage his horse train carried were a pen, ink, and paper. As with other travel accounts of this era, Traunter provided readers with factual reportage interlaced with a bit of fiction that he intended to publish as "The Travels of Richard Traunter on the Main Continent of America from Appomattox River in Virginia to Charles Town in South Carolina in the years 1698 and 1699." Unfortunately, his manuscript languished in the obscurity of private ownership for three hundred years, until it was acquired by the Virginia Museum of History and Culture in 2001.* This is the first time Traunter's narrative has been published. Only now are scholars beginning to appreciate how Traunter's *Travels* deepens our understanding of this tumultuous era. What makes *Travels* particularly interesting is that Traunter chronicled an environment and Native communities he knew well. The *Travels* is a three-hundred-year-old treasure that opens a new window into the late seventeenth-century Southeast.

WHO WAS RICHARD TRAUNTER?

So much about Traunter is a mystery. For centuries the only known mention of him was in England's Board of Trade records, where he appeared as one of six partners in the Board's Carolina silver scheme (1698–1700). The Board authorized the project after a "dealer" and a "planter" discovered silver in Carolina while in pursuit of "ennemy Indians." Traunter was the only partner considered a dealer.† His affidavit, or memorial, to the Board, presented jointly with Edward Loughton in July 1700, articulated how South Carolinians obstructed the partners' efforts to find the silver mine again, but the document said very little about Traunter himself.‡ The other colonists involved

---

* In 2001 the Traunter manuscript was donated to the Virginia Museum of History and Culture by the estate of Paul Mellon.

† The eight members of the Board of Trade who authorized the silver project were John Egerton, Earl of Bridgewater; Ford Grey, Earl of Tankerville; Sir Philip Meadows; John Locke; William Blathwayt; John Pollexfen; John Methuen; and Abraham Hill. Ex officio members were Charles Montagu, as Chancellor of the Exchequer; John Somers, Lord Keeper of the Seal; and Thomas Herbert, Earl of Pembroke, Lord Privy Seal. Bridgewater, Tankerville, Pembroke, Montagu, and Somers were also on King William III's Privy Council (Board of Trade, Representation to King William III, 18 April 1698; Board of Trade, Minute Book, 1698, 15).

‡ Loughton and Traunter, Memorial to the Board of Trade, appendix A in this work; the original document is in the United Kingdom's National Archives, Kew, Surrey.

INTRODUCTION

in the silver project were Loughton, an attorney who practiced in Charleston and London; and David Maybank, a Charleston resident.* Jean Couture, a *coureur des bois* once employed by René-Robert Cavelier, Sieur de LaSalle, and Henri Tonti at Arkansas Post, collaborated on the project but was not a partner.† The three other partners were based in London: William Good, Thomas Cutler, and John Smith. Good was in the service of Thomas Herbert, Earl of Pembroke, a Privy Counsellor to England's King William III.‡ Cutler and Smith were the front men who kept the Board up to date on the project's status. Smith was a member of Parliament, a Treasury lord, and a former Privy Counsellor to the king. He was politically allied with Charles Montagu, who was credited with the reformation of England's economic systems after the Nine Years' War—known in the colonies as King William's War—and the man to whom Traunter dedicated *Travels*.§ It is not known how Traunter came to know Smith or Montagu, men at the highest echelon of English politics, nor how Traunter first became acquainted with his other partners.

---

* Loughton was elected to the South Carolina Commons House of Assembly in 1703 and served until his death in 1707. He was related to Maybank by marriage and to London partner Thomas Cutler. According to Edward Randolph, surveyor-general of customs for England's North American colonies, Loughton and Maybank were "house carpenters" (Randolph to Bridgewater, 22 March 1698/1699, f. 77–77v). See also H. Smith, "Original Plan and the Earliest Settlers," 25; Withington, "South Carolina Gleanings in England," 289; Bates and Leland, *Proprietary Records of South Carolina*, 29, 119; Webber, "Hyrne Family," 102; Salley, *Journal of the Commons House of Assembly of South Carolina* (hereafter *JCHASC*) *1705/6*, 4; Salley, "Maybank Family," 115–16; Webber, "Bond Family of Hobcaw Plantation," 1–3.

† By 1696 Couture had allied himself with the English and owned property in South Carolina (Crane, *Southern Frontier*, 42–44). Couture, Letter, appendix D in this work. See also Ethridge, *From Chicaza to Chickasaw*, 150; Galloway, *Choctaw Genesis*, 175, 182.

‡ Board of Trade, Minute Book, 1698, 60. By 1703 Cutler must have had a Charleston residence, as the South Carolina Commons House of Assembly appointed him and Loughton to serve as "assessors" under the Act for the Keeping and Maintaining a Watch and Good Orders in Charles Town. The same year the assembly elected Cutler Messenger of the Commons, then rescinded the position when he failed to attend (McCord, *Statutes at Large*, 25; Salley, *JCHASC 1703*). Good died in South Carolina in the winter of 1698/1699 (Smith, Memorial to the Board of Trade, appendix B, 1–2, in this work; Smith, Abstract of the Proceedings relating to the Discovery of Silver Mines, appendix C, 1, in this work.) See also Jane Good, Will, 1 June 1702; Henry Good, Will, 13 January 1686.

§ Montagu developed the modern English economy, but Smith's political influence moved that legislation through Parliament (Horwitz, *Parliament, Policy and Politics*, 208; Speck, "Religion, Politics, and Society," 49–59; De Krey, *Fractured Society*, 26–27; Baxter, *Development of the Treasury*, 33, 138).

INTRODUCTION

The Travels of Richard Traunter includes frustratingly little personal information, but much can be learned about him from his colonial associates. Traunter oversaw the Indian trade business at Col. William Byrd's Appomattox store in Virginia. Byrd was elected to the Virginia House of Burgesses in 1677, served on the Governor's Council (1683–1704), and was Virginia's auditor-general (1688–1704), in which capacity he reported to the Board of Trade in London.* Traunter spent the winter of 1698–99 (the period between the two journals) in Charleston, seemingly as James Moore's houseguest. Moore, who became South Carolina's governor in 1700, made his fortune in the Indian slave trade. Traunter was also acquainted with two of Moore's accomplices in the Goose Creek political faction, Capt. Job Howes and Nathaniel Johnson; the latter became South Carolina's governor in 1703.† The man whom Traunter called "Indian Jack" may have been the enslaved man known as Wateree Jack who was attached to Moore's household.‡ Another Native man, Eno Will, traveled with Traunter for part of each journey.§ Two years later, in 1701, Will escorted John Lawson through what is today eastern North Carolina, and in 1733 he offered to lead William Byrd II to a silver mine.¶

Traunter was different from most of the men who worked as traders in England's North American colonies. He was an educated, moneyed man with political connections. Yet no personal or family records survive that show where or when Traunter was born, if he married and had children, or when he died. There is no trace of Traunter in property rolls or militia musters at

---

* J. L. Wright, *Only Land They Knew*, 106–7; Briceland, *Westward from Virginia*, 4; Tinling, *Correspondence of the Three William Byrds*, 1:3–4.

† Oatis, *Colonial Complex*, 35, 45; Edgar, *South Carolina*, 93.

‡ Indian Jack was a member of the Wateree tribe. Ivers says Moore's Indian slave known as Wateree Jack was emancipated by the time of the Yamasee War in 1715 and scouted for a South Carolina battalion that was ambushed. Some survivors accused Jack of duplicity, although there was no evidence to support the allegation. The first casualty of the Yamasee War was John Hearn, the man who escaped the attack that injured Indian Jack in 1697 (Ivers, *Torrent of Indians*, 86–88, 118; Traunter, *Travels*, preface, 8).

§ In 1698 Will joined Traunter's party from Occaneechi Town (at modern Hillsborough, North Carolina) to the Keyauwee Town (on Caraway Creek near present-day Asheboro, North Carolina). In 1699 Will led Traunter from Ajusher in the vicinity of today's Durham on a different route through North Carolina to modern Camden, South Carolina. For the locations of Occaneechi Town and Keyauwee Town, see Ward and Davis, "Tribes and Traders on the North Carolina Piedmont," 132; Beck, *Chiefdoms, Collapse*, 52.

¶ According to Merrell, the Eno Will whom John Lawson knew and the man Byrd II called Shacco-Will were the same man (Merrell, *Indians' New World*, 303n118; Lawson, *New Voyage*, 61–65; Byrd II, "Journey to the Land of Eden," in *Prose Works*, 382).

INTRODUCTION

a time when owning property and militia service defined colonial manhood. He had soldiering skills and participated in at least one military excursion, but it was common for traders to serve as adjuncts to colonial militia campaigns. Virginia archives that could shed light on Traunter no longer exist because he lived and worked in Virginia's "burned record counties," where few items survived the Civil War.[*] Byrd family materials pose another dead end. Byrd I's last letter-book entry was in August 1691. Traunter was employed by Byrd in 1697, perhaps earlier, but Byrd made few references to his employees.[†] Byrd's son, William Byrd II, did not mention Traunter either, although both Traunter and Byrd II knew Montagu.[‡]

What is known about Traunter raises other questions about his role and status in relation to the other traders Byrd employed, most of whom were considered "lower-class deerskin traders" who, Jessica Stern argues, kept the economy running but had no standing in colonial affairs.[§] There is very little documentary evidence for these men who were "the eyes and ears of the colonial governments" as they plied their wares in the southeastern interior. They were generally illiterate and marked their routes with "notches" and "scratchments" carved into trees, since fewer than a third of Englishmen could sign their names. Illiteracy was common in the late seventeenth century because it was economically determined. There were schools in prosperous parishes, but most had only one teacher, effectively limiting admission.[¶] English grammar schools instructed children from affluent families, but only a few charity institutions like London's Christ's Hospital educated poor or orphaned children.[**] Traunter could read and write, do math, and he knew a bit of Latin,

---

[*] The Library of Virginia, cited by Shefveland, *Anglo-Native Virginia*, 5. The absence of personal records for Traunter is common for this era in part because paper records are susceptible to damage by pests, water, fire, and neglect.

[†] In a 1700 deposition, Smith indicated that Traunter had been working among the Indians "for several years" (Smith memorial, appendix B, 4, in this work).

[‡] Montagu was president of the Royal Society when Byrd II was admitted. Byrd II purchased a replica of Michael Dahl's 1710 portrait of Montagu for his home at Westover, Virginia, which is now in the Virginia Museum of History and Culture's collection (Montagu, Portrait).

[§] Stern, *Lives in Objects*, 14.

[¶] Morris, *Bringing of Wonder*, 71; Briceland, "British Exploration of the United States Interior," 271; Merrell, *Indians' New World*, 28; Spufford, *Small Books and Pleasant Histories*, 21; Laslett, *World We Have Lost*, 229, 10.

[**] Byrd I asked his London agents to "procure" him "an ingenious youth that writes well" from Christ's Hospital, but Traunter was not that boy. Records for Christ's Hospital are complete, and no Richard Traunter, or even a Richard with compatible dates, appears

which points to some schooling. He was, in all likelihood, from a well-to-do family because he also had access to political elites like Smith and Montagu. And he had money. In vouching for his partners' "Good Credit," Smith cited each partner's annual income. Traunter's was the most substantial at £2,500 per annum, a figure far in excess of the £100 annual income attributed to each of the other partners.* That income level was, however, fairly ordinary for men from well-off English families. Nathaniel Bacon came to Virginia in 1674 with £1,800—enough to buy land in the colony and establish a business trading with the Indians. Colonial land ownership marked the difference between the "loose and disorderly" traders thought to have "no sense of allegiance to anyone but themselves" and planters whose property represented an investment in the colony's success. Because Traunter shared characteristics with both the traders and with the affluent planters, he may not have fit in with either class of men.†

Many property records for South Carolina exist, but despite his Charleston connections, there is no evidence that Traunter owned property there. Property ownership in the North Carolina colony is more difficult to verify since deeds were not registered until 1696, even though settlement began in the 1660s. An Edward Tranter purchased several hundred acres on the north side of the Pamlico River, but no title was entered until 1706. Edward Moseley's 1733 map of North Carolina noted Edward Tranter's residence on what is still known as Tranter's Creek.‡ In 1699 Richard Traunter visited that area on his way back to Virginia from Charleston. It may be coincidental that Richard Traunter went where Edward Tranter lived, but unrelated Traunters in the

---

in Hospital documents (Byrd I, Letter to Perry and Lane, in Tinling, *Correspondence*, 1:162; Mansell, *Christ's Hospital Pupils*).

* Cutler's status as a gentleman precluded a statement of wealth, as did Smith's political position. The average annual income for a gentleman was £280. That Traunter's income was ten times that amount suggests Traunter was a wealthy man (Hume, "Economics of Culture in London," 495; Smith memorial, appendix B, 4, in this work; Board of Trade, Representation to William III, f. 298–298v). It is unlikely that Smith exaggerated Traunter's income; he had such a reputation for being scrupulous that he was referred to as "Honest Jack Smith" (Baxter, *Development of the Treasury*, 138, 143).

† Rice, *Tales from a Revolution*, 27; Stern, "Economic Philosophies of Indian Trade," 97, 104.

‡ After an epidemic killed scores of Pamlico Indians in 1695, English settlers "moved south to occupy the peninsula between Albemarle Sound and the Pamlico River." Edward Tranter's property on Tranter's Creek was on this peninsula between the present-day towns of Robersonville and Washington, just northwest of Bath (Wood, "Changing Population," 68; John Tranter, Will; Norris, *Beaufort County, Deed Book I*, 31, 39; Moseley, *New and Correct Map of the Province of North Carolina*).

INTRODUCTION

relatively limited colonial population between Virginia and North Carolina seems unlikely. A subpoena issued to Edward Tranter in 1701 also implies a kinship tie between Richard and Edward. The subpoena compelled Edward to appear before the House of Lords as they considered a bill to revoke colonial proprietorships and establish a single administrative authority for all English colonies. It was issued just months after Richard Traunter testified before the English Board of Trade about South Carolinian recalcitrance toward the Crown. Two members of the House of Lords—the Earl of Stamford (Thomas Grey) and Lord Lexington (Robert Sutton)—served on the Board of Trade when Richard Traunter testified in 1700. Three others were involved in varying degrees with the Board's silver project that led to Traunter's testimony: John Egerton, the Earl of Bridgewater; Thomas Herbert, the Earl of Pembroke; and Charles Montagu, Lord Halifax.* The fact that the Lords turned to Edward Tranter instead of Richard Traunter is curious given Richard's extensive colonial experience and his prior official reportage to the Board of Trade, unless Richard was dead by the spring of 1701.

The Pamlico River was Tuscarora territory. Edward Tranter's property was nearly encircled by the Tuscaroras, who dominated commerce between Indians and the English in what is now eastern North Carolina. In *A New Voyage to Carolina* (1709), John Lawson wrote, "The *Tuskeruro's* are the most numerous in *North Carolina,* therefore their Tongue is understood by some in every Town of all the *Indians* near us." It was also one of the three Indigenous languages Richard Traunter spoke. The other two languages—Wateree and Waxhaw—aided Virginians' transactions with Indians in the southern piedmont. The South Carolina colony had very little intercourse with these Native peoples until the end of the seventeenth century. The first recorded interaction between Charleston and upcountry Indians occurred when a delegation of Esaws, Congarees, and Waxhaws visited Charleston in 1692. By that time Virginians had trucked goods into Carolina's Indigenous communities for over three decades.† Traunter's linguistic skills were an asset that contributed to Byrd I's dominance and profitability in the trade with southeastern Indians. Byrd's traders brought their skins and furs to Traunter at the Appomattox

---

* The subpoena for Edward Tranter to testify in relation to An Act for re-uniting to the Crown the Government of Several Colonies and Plantations in *America* was issued on a Saturday for the following Monday, suggesting that he was in London. The hearing was never conducted. Whatever information the Lords wanted from Tranter remains unknown (*Journal of the House of Lords,* 16:713–15).

† Lawson, *New Voyage,* 233; La Vere, *Tuscarora War,* 43; Merrell, *Indians' New World,* 55.

INTRODUCTION

store, as did area Indians. But there was no advantage for Waterees or Waxhaws to travel hundreds of miles north when Virginians brought merchandise into their towns. Traunter must have made regular excursions to them, which, in addition to his fluency in their languages, explains his familiarity with the road networks that connected Indian communities. Native customs established late winter as the season when non-Indians were welcome in Indigenous towns. Restricting the trade season meant that "the rest of the year, natives had the interior virtually to themselves." As winter approached, Virginia traders clustered around the Appomattox store where Traunter worked and waited for the "grains of Mayze, or small stones" that Indians sent to invite traders into their towns and villages. Around 1700 Virginia traders began to increasingly defy the Indians' conventions. They stopped waiting for the invitation and entered the piedmont whenever they wanted, as Traunter did when he traveled in the late summer and early autumn.*

So, who was Richard Traunter? Despite what can be gleaned from the *Travels*, he remains enigmatic. No known evidence exists that tells us how long he lived in Virginia or if he lived in South Carolina before he worked for Colonel Byrd. His associations in both Charleston and Virginia, as well as his familiarity with Indians throughout the Southeast—his ability to speak Waxhaw as well as Tuscarora—make it difficult to determine whether he considered himself a Virginian or a Carolinian, North or South. One thing is clear. He believed his journeys contributed "to the common Good" of his country, a sentiment consistent with imperialists who thought "a peaceful trade would build a stronger empire."†

THE NATIVE SOUTHEAST

The Native Southeast that Traunter traveled through was inhabited by Siouan, Algonquian, and Iroquoian peoples whose roots in the region stretched back centuries and millennia. Cactus Hill, located on Virginia's Nottoway River, is one of the oldest human habitation sites in North America with artifacts from 18,000 to 20,000 years old.‡ During the Mississippian period (900–1700 CE),

---

* Merrell, "Our Bond of Peace," 284, 278.

† Traunter, *Travels*, preface, 7, and title page; Hall, *Zamumo's Gifts*, 112.

‡ Cactus Hill is roughly 45 miles south of Richmond near Stony Creek in Sussex County, Virginia: see Johnson, "Cactus Hill Archaeology Site," *Encyclopedia Virginia*; McAvoy, "Analysis of Woodland and Historic Period Occupation," 279–80; McAvoy and McAvoy, *Archaeological Investigations*, 10, 16.

southeastern Indians built cities and towns whose substantial populations shaped regional economies and cultures. Cahokia, for instance, located east of present-day St. Louis, had a twelfth-century population of 38,000 and was "the most densely populated site in aboriginal North America." Towns and ceremonial centers throughout the Southeast featured sophisticated scientific structures such as celestial observatories and astronomical calendars.* Southeastern Indians organized themselves into sovereign chiefdoms that varied in size and territorial influence. The political authority of paramount chiefdoms was far-flung, covering several hundred miles, with several subordinate chiefdoms providing the paramount polity with tribute. Simple chiefdoms controlled more modest orbits that had clusters of four to seven towns in which 350 to 650 people lived. Cofitachequi (near modern Camden, South Carolina) was a paramount chiefdom whose domain in the sixteenth and seventeenth centuries included the Siouan towns of the Esaws, Waterees, Sugarees, Catawbas, Waxhaws, Congarees, and Santees.†

By the late sixteenth century, the Algonquians of Tsenacommacah, in what is today Virginia, were governed by a paramount chief, or *mamanatowick*, whose jurisdiction of at least eight towns—Powhatan, Arrohateck, Appamattuck, Pamunkey, Mattaponi, Chiskiack, Youghtanund, and the capital town of Werowocomoco on the York River—stretched a hundred miles from the north side of Chesapeake Bay southward to today's border with North Carolina and a hundred miles inland from the Atlantic coast.‡ Ossomocomuck, a separate Algonquian domain to the south, had self-governing *weroances* (district chiefs) who each controlled a few towns in the North Carolina Sounds region from Roanoke Island westward through the Pamlico and Chowan river basins. Farther inland, roughly fifteen autonomous Tuscarora (Iroquois) towns dotted the waterways of eastern North Carolina at the end of the seventeenth century. Tuscarora communities were led by a *teetha*, who implemented the consensual decisions of the village council. Europeans, Phillip Round reminds us, entered a Southeast with "complex Indigenous

---

* Oatis, *Colonial Complex*, 13; C. Hudson, *Southeastern Indians*, 77.

† Ethridge and Mitchem, "Interior South at the Time of Spanish Exploration," 170–71; Widmer, "Structure of Southeastern Chiefdoms," 126–27; J. L. Wright, *Only Land*, 119. See also C. Hudson, *Southeastern Indians*, 202, 191.

‡ Rountree argues that "the Algonquian-speaking ethnic groups of the James, the York, and probably the Rappahannock river basins were chiefdoms fully integrated into Powhatan's 'empire'—which was *not* a 'confederacy'" (*Pocahontas's People*, 10, 3–4; Rountree and Turner, *Before and After Jamestown*, 36; Rountree, *Powhatan Indians of Virginia*, 106).

geopolitical alliances that determined how Europeans would encounter both the New World and its peoples."*

Exchanges between Indigenous people, as James Merrell explains, were rooted in alliances that brought outsiders into "a web of kinship that lay at the foundation of native life." One way to form a kinship alliance was for outsiders to marry into a community. For Indians, the marriage represented the outsider's willingness to adhere to "local forms of social control" and the "traditional rules governing inter-personal relations."† In southeastern societies, gifting rituals facilitated the transfer of "marriage partners, resources, labor, ideas, techniques, and religious practices" through an extensive infrastructure of roads that connected Indigenous towns and villages across the continent.‡ Indians living in the Southeast used the trail systems to trade with Native peoples in the Great Lakes and the Great Plains from whom they obtained "high-prestige trade objects"—copper and marine shell—in exchange for mica, deerskins, and turkey feathers. The pathways also functioned as "historical documents, serving as mnemonic devices for recalling significant elements of past individual and collective experience" as well as metaphorical representations of human "movement through a moral universe" that "link[ed] the past with the present, and life with death."§ The routes were ample structures that accommodated the armies and livestock herds that accompanied Europeans who came to the Southeast in search of gold and slaves.

When Spaniards entered the Southeast, James Taylor Carson reminds us, they were utterly dependent upon Indigenous assistance, or, at the least, acquiescence. Spanish expeditions did not carry sufficient provisions for themselves because they assumed Indians would feed them and their animals.

---

* Oberg, *Head in Edward Nugent's Hand*, 2–3; La Vere, *Tuscarora War*, 44, 43; Round, "Mississippian Contexts," 453.

† Merrell, "Our Bond of Peace," 279. European travelers often misunderstood the cultural purpose of marriage alliances. Lawson, for instance, associated Indian "trading Girls" with prostitutes and identified an Indian headman who extended the kinship offer as a "Bawd" (*New Voyage*, 192, 41). During his boundary survey, Byrd II wrote that the Weyanoke Indians "offered us no bedfellows, according to the good Indian fashion," which he and his companions "took unkindly" (Byrd II, "Secret History of the Line," in *Prose Works*, 82).

‡ Salisbury, "Indians' Old World," 5–6. See also Stern, *Lives in Objects*, 96–97.

§ Ethridge, "Navigating the Mississippian World," 64–65; Waselkov, "Exchange and Interaction since 1500," 14:642; Kelton, *Epidemics and Enslavement*, 40; Fitts, "Mapping Catawba Coalescence," 16. See also Nabokov, "Orientations from Their Side," 264; Tanner, "Land and Water Communication Systems," 28–30, 32.

INTRODUCTION

When Pánfilo de Narváez (1528) and Hernando de Soto (1539–42) penetrated the Southeast's interior, they expected "compliant native peoples" to bestow "all they owned upon them with selfless generosity" in exchange for the "gift" of baptism. The *Requerimiento* of 1513, a verbal warning for Indians to convert to Christianity or endure "all the evil and damages" of slavery and war, also negated, even forbade, alliances with non-Christians.* At Cofitachequi, a town with imposing structures, temples, and fruit-laden orchards, Soto and his men were met by its paramount chief, a young woman carried on a linen-draped litter, who greeted Soto with a necklace of pearls and other luxury goods. Soto accepted the gifts but spurned the alliance they offered. He looted Cofitachequi's temples, desecrated funerary sites, and confiscated the town's food stores. Other Native towns were ransacked as Soto continued through the Southeast, leaving a "trail of shattered lives, broken bodies, ravaged fields, empty storehouses, and charred villages." When Native people resisted Soto's onslaught, they were "thrown to the dogs, or burned alive."† Juan Pardo's attempts to establish six small garrisons in 1566 failed in part because of Soto's legacy and because the Spaniards offered no reciprocal benefit in goods or services, so Indians stopped feeding Pardo's men. The Spaniards' coastal forts fared somewhat better, although Lucas Vásquez de Ayllón's colony of six hundred persons at San Miguel de Gualdape (1526), in what is now Georgia, lasted mere months, as did the Jesuit mission at Ajacán (1570) in Powhatan territory near the Chesapeake Bay. Pedro Menéndez de Avilés's fort of St. Augustine (1565) in Florida, and Santa Elena (1566) on today's Parris Island, South Carolina, lasted longer. But by 1587 only St. Augustine was still a functioning Spanish settlement. Many of the towns the Spanish decimated, including Cofitachequi, rebounded. When Charleston's Henry Woodward visited in 1670, Cofitachequi still received tribute from nearby chiefs.‡

Englishmen were also in pursuit of "profit, empire, and Christianity" when, in 1584, they ventured onto Roanoke Island off the coast of present-day North Carolina. Wingina and Granganimeo—two *weroances* of Ossomocumuck—treated the newcomers as guests and initiated the ritual of exchange that transformed Philip Amadas, Arthur Barlowe, and the rest of their company

---

* Carson, *Making an Atlantic World,* 49; Oberg and Moore, "Voyages to Carolina," 47–48; Seed, *Ceremonies of Possession,* 69.

† Cofitachequi is now the Mulberry archaeology site. Beck, *Chiefdoms, Collapse,* 66–67; C. Hudson, *Southeastern Indians,* 109; Weber, *Spanish Frontier,* 51–52.

‡ Oberg and Moore, "Voyages to Carolina," 45–46; Weber, *Spanish Frontier,* 69–75, 87, 90; Bowne, "Dr. Henry Woodward's Role," 75.

INTRODUCTION

"from strangers to kin."* Wingina settled the Englishmen on the north side of the island, where he could keep an eye on their interactions with his Native rivals and allies. He also introduced the English visitors to other Algonquians. Ralph Lane, Thomas Hariot, and John White were taken to Chesapeake Bay where they spent the winter of 1584–85 as guests of Powhatan Indians. Relations soured between the Algonquians and English on Roanoke Island after an outbreak of disease prompted Wingina to move his people to the safety of Dasemunkepeuc, a village on the mainland. The English took affront, stormed Dasemunkepeuc, and killed Wingina. In what the Indians considered a particularly savage act, Ralph Lane took Wingina's head as a trophy. Algonquians throughout the region were outraged. Wahunsenacawh, the *mamanatowick* of Tsenacommacah, whom the English called Powhatan, led the retaliatory raid that destroyed the colony. Supply ships in 1588 found Roanoke Island deserted.†

Not surprisingly, Wahunsenacawh wanted nothing to do with the English who, as guests of the *weroance* of Paspihe in 1607, set themselves up on an island they called Jamestown. Wahunsenacawh refused to meet there with Capt. John Smith. Doing so would have legitimized English occupation of the island, and Wahunsenacawh saw no reason to "undertake the long-term feeding of sizeable numbers of European visitors." Smith made matters worse when he asked Algonquians to betray their allegiance to Wahunsenacawh and align with him instead. A detente was reached, and food was given to the newcomers, after Wahunsenacawh obtained the English weaponry he wanted to maintain Powhatan advantage against his Siouan adversaries, the Monacans and the Mannahoacs.‡ Conflict erupted in 1622 when colonists

---

* Wingina later took the name Pemisapan (Oberg and Moore, "Voyages to Carolina," 53, 37, 21, 49–50). Amadas and Barlowe described Roanoke as a "delicate garden" with "unimproved" lands—property without fences, livestock, tillage, or manured fields—the lack of which, in English law, allowed for English expropriation (qtd. in Seed, *Ceremonies of Possession*, 25–26).

† Oberg and Moore, "Voyages to Carolina," 49–51, 53; Rountree, *Pocahontas's People*, 20. Dasemunkepeuc was located in the vicinity of today's Mann's Harbor, North Carolina (Oberg, *Head in Edward Nugent's Hand*, 6, 11). Wahunsenacawh is also spelled as Wahunsonacock. Lane's savage act of taking Wingina's head was in keeping with English customs to display the heads of traitors on London Bridge.

‡ Carson, *Making an Atlantic World*, 58, 61; Merrell, "Second Thoughts," 478; Rountree and Turner, *Before and After Jamestown*, 22; Rountree, *Powhatan Indians*, 120–22; Rountree, "Trouble Coming Southward," 65–66. See also Capt. John Smith, *Generall Historie of Virginia*, in Castillo and Schweitzer, *Literatures of Colonial America*, 199.

moved deeper into the Virginia mainland in defiance of established boundaries. Opechancanough, who became *mamanatowick* after Wahunsenacawh's death, sacked the English enclave at Martin's Hundred and killed most of its inhabitants. The English were undeterred. Over the next two decades they expanded their footprint from the Tidewater to the fall line, deep in the Powhatan homeland. By the mid-seventeenth century Virginia colonists had displaced the Powhatans—as well as the Weyanokes and Nansemonds—from the Tidewater region and relegated Indians to lands "eastward from the Monacan town above the James River Falls to the head of Blackwater River (near modern-day Franklin, Virginia)."* Near the former Powhatan town of Arrohateck, the Virginians erected Fort Henrico in 1650. From there, Abraham Wood, Cadwallader Jones, and Thomas Stegge (Byrd I's uncle) began a brisk business supplying English goods to Indians in exchange for their war prisoners.†

Up and down the Atlantic coast, encroachments displaced the Southeast's Indigenous people and triggered Anglo-Indian violence, as well as Indian-Indian hostilities, in ways that altered the region's human landscape. In the 1650s, for example, intra-Iroquoian tensions prompted the Westo Indians to migrate from their Iroquoian homelands on Lake Erie to the falls of the James River in Virginia. The proximity of the six hundred or so Westo "strangers" alarmed English colonists, even though the Westos lived there peaceably. The Westos defended themselves against an unprovoked Virginia militia campaign, a conflict that the settlers termed the Battle of Bloody Run, then relocated to South Carolina's Savannah River to avoid repercussions. After settling themselves in the South, the Westos implemented their Iroquoian practice of waging war specifically to obtain slaves that they exchanged with Virginia traders for arms and ammunition.‡ Iroquoian kinships were sustained by mourning wars that, according to Daniel Richter, were "a principal means of coping with the death of loved ones." In skirmishes with traditional enemies, Iroquoians obtained captives that were either adopted by grieving families as an "almost literal replacement" for lost loved ones or were executed to revenge the loss. War captives were also an integral part of Native southeastern cultures. Adopted captives "held the same rights as a birth

---

* Rountree and Turner, *Before and After Jamestown*, 149–50; J. L. Wright, *Only Land*, 84–85; Rountree, "Trouble Coming Southward," 70–71.

† Briceland, *Westward from Virginia*, 3–4; Bowne, "Bold and Warlike People," 125–27.

‡ Beck, *Chiefdoms, Collapse*, 15, 114–15; Bowne, *Westo Indians*, 77–80.

member" of the tribe. Slaves, on the other hand, were "a sort of living scalp" who performed menial work for their captors.* According to Lawson, the word Indians used to denote "slave" was the same word used for "domestick Beasts," or "any other thing of that Nature, which is obsequiously to depend on the Master for its Sustenance." Life for Indian slaves could be precarious but bore no resemblance to the chattel slavery promulgated by English colonists. To increase profitability, tobacco plantations in the mid-seventeenth century increasingly relied on the labor of the Indian slaves that Virginia traders obtained from the Westos. Charleston was founded in 1670 and gave the Westos another market for their slaves—until 1680, when Carolinians forcibly displaced the Westos to gain control of the Indian slave trade in the southern piedmont. Nathaniel Bacon waged a similar campaign against the Occaneechis in 1676, and for the same purpose: to increase profits by removing the slave trade's Native middlemen.†

In the ensuing decades, slave raids disrupted the continuity of Native life in the Southeast. Robin Beck reasons that the Westo and Occaneechi slave raiders dismantled the Mississippian chiefdoms, including Cofitachequi. The slave trade also spread smallpox, an "epidemiological catastrophe" that caused depopulation over the course of weeks rather than years or centuries. Smallpox was in two of the three southernmost communities Traunter visited in 1698—the Suterees and the Waxhaws. Indians' lack of previous exposure meant that nearly everyone in an infected town contracted the disease, about 30 percent of whom died. Archaeologists have learned that in some hard-hit communities the disease interrupted traditional burial practices. Many of the dead were "lowered into shallow graves that were left empty of the goods that customarily traveled with the departing spirit." There were too few people well enough to tend to the sick and bury the dead.‡

The late seventeenth century was a period of ethnogenesis, defined by Richter and Merrell as "the making and remaking of Native nations that went on in response to the disease, displacement, and dispossession" caused by

---

* Richter, "Ordeals of the Longhouse," 16; Holm, "American Indian Warfare," 156–57; Morris, *Bringing of Wonder*, 77; C. Hudson, *Southeastern Indians*, 254.

† Lawson, *New Voyage*, 210; Bowne, "Bold and Warlike," 127; Bowne, "Henry Woodward's Role," 75; J. L. Wright, *Only Land*, 107, 105; Rice, "Bacon's Rebellion," 738. Waselkov notes that "large numbers of enslaved Indians were sent to the Caribbean in the aftermath of Bacon's Rebellion," including Occaneechis ("Exchange and Interaction," 688).

‡ Beck, *Chiefdoms, Collapse*, 15, 44; C. Hudson, *Southeastern Indians*, 105; Merrell, "Our Bond of Peace," 273. See also Kelton, "Great Southeastern Smallpox Epidemic," 21.

smallpox and the slave trade. Some Native communities were remade through coalescence, a process whereby dislocated peoples reformed themselves into a new community. Ajusher, where Eno Will was the "chief Man," was a coalescent community visited by Traunter and Lawson. Lawson identified "*Will's Nation*" as "*Shoccories*, mixt with the *Enoe-Indians*, and those of the Nation of *Adshusheer.*" Traunter encountered Acamantiaes and Saponis living there as well.* Will is featured prominently in Traunter's narrative. He is also one of the few Native men who appears with some specificity in more than one colonial account. In "Journey to the Land of Eden" (1733), Byrd II said Will was seventy-eight years old, which means he was born about 1655 and was in his midforties when he traveled with Traunter and Lawson. Will told Lawson that he had lived at "*Enoe*-Bay" on the Eno River as a boy, but no more. Traunter did not say, and may not have known, if the deserted Eno Fields he visited on the "Geniton-Tarr River" was the place Will called Enoe-Bay. According to Traunter, Tuscaroras ransacked Eno Fields after which Eno survivors found refuge with Shakoris. In 1698 Will lived with the Occaneechis.†

Tuscarora country was just east of where the Occaneechis lived after 1680. David La Vere describes Tuscaroras as the southern "tip of an Iroquoian arrow pointed at the heart of North Carolina's" Siouan peoples, but it was Senecas who posed the greatest threat to Siouans in the Southeast. Senecas were one of the five Iroquois nations of the Haudenosaunee, a political confederacy whose northeastern territorial dominance extended from the Great Lakes to the Atlantic coast before and during the colonial era.‡ Why Seneca-

---

* Richter and Merrell, preface to *Beyond the Covenant Chain*, xiii; Ethridge and Hudson quoted in Beck, *Chiefdoms, Collapse*, 7; Lawson, *New Voyage*, 61–62; Traunter, *Travels*, Journal One, 23. See also Davis and Ward, "Evolution of Siouan Communities," 52. Traunter visited Ajusher in 1699, but mentioned them in his journal for 1698, grouping the Ajusheres with the the Enos, Saponis, Shockoris, and the Acamantiaes. The name Acamantiae may be a phonetic variation of Aramanchee or Aramancy. The Aramanchee River, now known as Great Alamance Creek in North Carolina, was variously recorded as Aramancy and Aramanchy on maps by Joshua Fry and Peter Jefferson (1755) and Henry Popple (1733): see Fry and Jefferson, *Map of the Most Inhabited Part of Virginia . . . and North Carolina*; Popple, *Map of the British Empire*.

† Byrd II, "Journey to the Land of Eden," in *Prose Works*, 382; Lawson, *New Voyage*, 63. Traunter located Eno Fields by the "Geniton-Tarr River," but no river of that name exists. Lawson used the term Iroquois interchangeably with "Sinnagers" and "Jennitos," which bear a phonetic similarity to "Geniton" (Traunter, *Travels*, Journal One, 18; Lawson, *New Voyage*, 53).

‡ La Vere, *Tuscarora War*, 40. The other four Haudenosaunee nations were the Mohawks, Onondagas, Oneidas, and Cayugas. The Tuscaroras lived in North Carolina until

INTRODUCTION

Siouan hostilities began, or precisely when, is unknown, but Senecas considered piedmont Indians their "ancient enemies." Archaeological evidence uncovered by Stephen Davis and Trawick Ward indicates northern Iroquois campaigns against southeastern Siouan peoples began by the fifteenth century. Seneca warfare traditionally occurred in the spring and summer. That changed after the Siouan-Occaneechis attacked Iroquoian-Susquehannocks as they fled Bacon's vigilantes in 1676. After the Susquehannock survivors returned to the northern fold, Seneca aggressions became a year-round threat: "Iroquois warriors menaced every piedmont town." A series of Seneca assaults on Occaneechee Island in 1681 forced the Occaneechis to abandon their island for modern Hillsborough, North Carolina, where Traunter and Lawson found them in 1698 and 1701, respectively.*

Virginia colonists were alarmed by the damage Senecas inflicted on the Siouans. Cadwallader Jones cited a battle in 1682 when some Senecas "took from an Indian town 35 [people] and 4 or 5 [others] from several small towns ... probably in Catawba country." For many Virginians, "just the sight of random war parties sent shivers down the spines," even though Senecas rarely harmed English colonists. Fear of Seneca predation, fueled by intermittent destruction of English livestock, lingered in the colonial imagination to such an extent that into the eighteenth century it "acted as a brake on Virginia's, and the empire's, expansion."† Cairns along the roadways were visible reminders of the dangers Senecas posed to the region. At Yadkin Ford, Lawson described how his Indian guide added a stone to each of seven "monuments" for those "slain in that place by the *Sinnagers,* or *Iroquois.*" At the "great heaps of stones" Traunter encountered between Eno Fields and the Occaneechi town, he mentioned a similar ritual whereby each Indian is bound "to cast a stone to the heap ... and noe more."‡

It is unclear how long Eno Will lived with the Occaneechis, but he was

---

the Tuscarora War (1711–13), after which they migrated to New York and joined the Haudenosaunee (Dunbar-Ortiz, *Indigenous Peoples' History,* 24, 76).

* Merrell, "Their Very Bones Shall Fight," 116; Davis and Ward, "Evolution of Siouan Communities," 40; Merrell, *Indians' New World,* 41, 42.

† In a rare exception, Iroquoians killed six of Byrd I's traders who were returning to Virginia from Carolina in 1684. That same year, though, a party of fifty Senecas passed through Byrd's property at the James River Falls without incident (Briceland, "It has been long our policy," 499; Beck, *Chiefdoms, Collapse,* 170; Rhoades, *Long Knives and the Longhouse,* 39, 75).

‡ Lawson, *New Voyage,* 50; Traunter, *Travels,* Journal One, 18.

INTRODUCTION

doubtless aware of their altercations with the Senecas, and Bacon, that contributed to their diminished regional status. Merrell reasons that by the time Will befriended Lawson, he "had fallen into the limbo of native society" and was "a marginal member of colonial life." Evidence for Will's peripheral role is based in part on his fear, told to Lawson, "of being poison'd by some wicked *Indians*" because he was "always ready to serve the *English*." Traunter sheds new light on Will's position in the Native southeast that supports Lawson's assertion that, from Ajusher, Will "rules as far as the Banks of *Reatkin*," or Yadkin River. According to Traunter, Will had sufficient political authority to insert himself into civic affairs at the Keyauwee town on Caraway Creek, well to the west in North Carolina, and at a remote Waxhaw village located just north of present-day Camden, South Carolina. Traunter wrote that Indians respected Will more than all the other "kings" in the Southeast and equated Will's clout to that of Aurangzeb, the sixth Mughal emperor of India, who declared war on the English East India Company in response to English pirates' rapaciousness in 1695.* Will's "Coat of party-coloured Red and blew Cloth, with Copper Lace" is consistent with clothing worn by privileged persons. Michael Oberg argues that "only *weroances* and their closest advisors" wore copper.† Both Traunter and Lawson represent Will as a "chief man" who managed his associations with English colonists while he maintained his leadership role at Ajusher and his alliances with at least five other Native peoples in the Southeast—Occaneechis, Keyauwees, Saxapahaws, Waxhaws, and Tuscaroras.

Eno Will's relationship with the Tuscaroras may have been complicated. Will conducted Lawson through Tuscarora lands in 1701 without incident. For an unknown reason, however, Will furnished Traunter with a convoy of "Six Indian Hunters" as he and Traunter's four men went from Ajusher to the Haw River. How close Traunter came to Tuscarora country depends on where he crossed the Haw River and how far east he was, since the Tuscarora homelands were to the southeast of Haw River, from along the Roanoke River to Contentnea Creek and the Neuse River.‡ Traunter and Will moved

---

* Merrell, *Indians' New World*, 44; Lawson, *New Voyage*, 62; Traunter, *Travels*, Journal One, 23, and Journal Two, 48–49; Hanna, "Protecting the Rights of Englishmen," 303–4.

† Traunter, *Travels*, Journal Two, 39; Oberg, *Head in Edward Nugent's Hand*, 46.

‡ Traunter, *Travels*, Journal Two, 43; La Vere, *Tuscarora War*, 16, 3. It is strange that Traunter would avoid the Tuscaroras since he had ongoing trade with them at the Appomattox store (Palmer, *Calendar of Virginia State Papers*, 65).

INTRODUCTION

southward, passing east of the Uwharrie Mountains either through or around Tuscarora territory. After John Lederer's excursion in 1670 to the Tuscarora town of "Katearas"—probably Catechna at modern Grifton, North Carolina— few Englishmen ventured into this region. Tuscaroras had good reasons to be suspicious of Englishmen in their backyard. Like their Occaneechi neighbors, the Tuscaroras were targeted by Charleston slave raiders coming from the south and west in the 1690s. They also had to contend with increasing numbers of English settlers on their coastal lands. These factors may have influenced Will's movement through what is now eastern North Carolina as he guided Traunter toward South Carolina on what Traunter boasted was a "new discover'd roade." It must have been a road Will used often, as he was well known in the remote Waxhaw village Traunter stumbled on in today's Kershaw or Chesterfield County in South Carolina. Will's presence in Traunter's party kept interactions with the Waxhaws amiable, but Traunter's gifts, given by Will after Traunter left the village, suggest a transgression occurred that Will patched up. There are hints, as well, that Will had not intended to take Traunter to this village.*

South of the Tuscaroras and north of the Waxhaw village, Will led Traunter along a trail that ran from modern Fayetteville, North Carolina, to Town Creek, a Mississippian ceremonial center near present-day Mount Gilead, North Carolina. In excavations of Town Creek, archaeologist Edmond Boudreaux unearthed glass trade beads manufactured between 1500 and 1800 as well as a burial site that dated to 1746. He concluded that Town Creek was, at the very least, intermittently occupied through the eighteenth century. Joffre Coe, in earlier archaeological excavations, had uncovered early nineteenth-century documents noting that Indians moved between Town Creek and Fayetteville on what may have been the same pathway Traunter took or a parallel one.† Traunter made no mention of the Town Creek site. Nor did he directly reference Cofitachequi, which he passed within a few miles of when he went from the remote Waxhaw village to Camden. He noted, though, that the people in that remote village considered themselves a "remnant of Waxawes" who, as J. Leitch Wright points out, were themselves remnants of the Cofitachequi chiefdom. Traunter may not have fully understood the history of the

---

* Lederer, *Discoveries of John Lederer*, 162; La Vere, *Tuscarora War*, 37, 16; Traunter, *Travels*, Journal Two, 48–50.
† Boudreaux, *Archaeology of Town Creek*, 62; Coe, *Town Creek Indian Mound*, 37.

INTRODUCTION

areas he traveled through. He recognized, obliquely, that the "new" road had long been used by Native people when he claimed to be the "first man of his Majesties Subjects (or of any other Christian)" to use it. Like many Europeans who came to the Southeast before and after him, Traunter's "discoveries" were made possible with the assistance of southeastern Indians, especially Eno Will. It is important, therefore, to read Traunter's account through its Native context, to remember that it was Will and the Southeast's Indigenous peoples who controlled how Traunter engaged with them and their environments.[*]

WHY TRAUNTER TRAVELED

Traunter gave three reasons for his journeys: to satisfy his intellectual curiosity, to make peace with Indians, and to seek revenge. He had other motives as well: to re-locate a silver source for the Board of Trade and find a shorter route between Virginia and South Carolina. The Board of Trade and William III authorized the silver project after Traunter and Loughton had stumbled on silver ore "on the very surface of the Earth" a few years earlier.[†] Seven of the eleven men who left Appomattox River with Traunter in 1698 were identified as Traunter's "own men": that is, men who were likely involved in the silver project. The other four were traders working for Byrd I who were headed for the Esaws. Traunter's seven men included, in all probability, Edward Loughton and David Maybank, both project partners, and Solomon Legaré, a Charleston silversmith who was affiliated with the endeavor but not a partner.[‡] Also in the party were Henry Netherton, a planter-surveyor from Westmoreland County, Virginia;[§] Indian Jack, an Indian slave Traunter was remanding to James Moore in Charleston; and Traunter's servant, most likely an Indian slave. Traunter named these men either in a deposition he and Loughton delivered to the Board of Trade or in *Travels*. The identity

---

[*] Traunter, *Travels*, Journal Two, 49; J. L. Wright, *Only Land*, 119; Traunter, *Travels*, preface, 7; Round, "Mississippian Contexts," 450.

[†] Board of Trade, Minute Book, 1698, 60.

[‡] Traunter, *Travels*, Journal One, 11. Maybank, Legaré, and Netherton are listed in the Traunter-Loughton deposition, as is Jean Couture. It is tempting to think that Couture was the unnamed man, but that is unlikely given the sequence of events Couture relates in his letter to the Board. Legaré, identified as a silversmith/goldsmith, was probably the Frenchman in the party (Ruymbeke, *From New Babylon to Eden*, 203–4, 288n22; Loughton and Traunter memorial, appendix A in this work).

[§] Netherton also witnessed land transactions in Charles County, Maryland; Fothergill, *Wills of Westmoreland County*, 62; Tucker, *Colonial Virginians*, 39, 43.

INTRODUCTION

of the seventh man is a mystery.* Only four men went with Traunter in 1699: most likely Legaré, Netherton, a servant, and an unknown man. Eno Will, and Will's servant, accompanied Traunter for a portion of both treks.†

In the course of his second expedition, Traunter and his companions created a wooden "monument," in what is now Lancaster County, South Carolina. They roped a log to the top of a tree so that it was "poysed in the Ayr" some twenty feet up, presumably to stake claim to a silver mine there. The log was inscribed with the date, the men's names, and even the number of horses they had with them.‡ Similar marks signaled ownership of the "new discover'd roade" they had taken from Ajusher, a road that crossed the main Waxhaw road near modern Camden, South Carolina. The groundwork for his "discovery" of the "new" road was laid during Traunter's 1698 trip when he deviated from the main trade route to search for other ways to the Waxhaws. His journals suggest he found one near the Indian towns of Occaneechi and Ajusher, and another by Keyauwee.§ Traunter stressed the utility of the new, safer passageway between Virginia and South Carolina. This was

---

* Indian Jack and Traunter's "man," a term Traunter used for a servant, were recorded in Traunter, *Travels*, preface, 10, and Journal One, 11. Traunter likewise described Eno Will's servant as Will's "man" (Traunter, *Travels*, Journal One, 22).

† During Traunter's second trip in the fall of 1699, Loughton and Maybank were in Charleston, as was Indian Jack.

‡ Traunter described building the monument at "Doubtful Branch" but did not reference it as a discovery as he did the road (Traunter, *Travels*, Journal Two, 47–48). Lancaster County's immense silver and gold deposits produced millions of dollars of ore annually well into the twentieth century (Pardee and Park, "Map of the Central Piedmont Region of North Carolina and South Carolina," in Roberts, *Carolina Gold Rush*; Dahlberg, "Common Good of My Country," 331–33). In 1799 the discovery of a seventeen-pound chunk of gold lying on open ground at John Reed's farm in Cabarrus County, North Carolina, triggered a gold rush in the piedmont region. Traunter's monument was located just a few miles south of Reed's farm and even nearer to what became the Brewer Gold Mine and the Haile Gold Mine, both of which produced enormous quantities of silver and gold (Roberts, *Carolina Gold Rush*, 5–6; Williams, *Georgia Gold Rush*, 3, 8, 107).

§ Traunter deviated from the main trade road at least seven times in 1698. At Nottoway River, for example, Traunter and one companion got "lost" hunting, forcing an overnight stay. The 20-mile round trip from this location to the rest of his party was equivalent to a full day of travel but was not included in his mileage. The longest deviation from the main trade road—some 73 miles—was in South Carolina between the Wateree Indians and Hanging Rock east of the main Waxhaw road. The *soc-ca-hick* Traunter gave Eno Will required the Indians at Keyauwee, Occaneechi, and Ajusher to give traders safe passage, suggesting there were nearby access points to the "new" road by these towns (Traunter, *Travels*, Journal One, 13–14).

a decidedly Virginian perspective since, as Stephen Feeley shows, Virginia and South Carolina were engaged in a fierce competition for "Indian trading partners," and South Carolina resented the presence of Virginia pack trains in the Carolinas, some of which had more than two hundred horses loaded with great quantities of trade goods used to "poach 'their' Indian clients."* The two colonies fought to control the Indian slave trade, which Traunter's new road facilitated. The new road also represented a secret way to move goods between the Virginia and Charleston—Indian slaves, horses, and, potentially, silver.†

Byrd I and Moore—the two men Traunter shuttled between on his expeditions—dominated the Indian slave trade in their respective colonies after the Occaneechi and Westo middlemen were displaced in the 1670s. Both men were motivated by profit. One Indian slave was worth two hundred deerskins, which was half as much as English indentured servants or African slaves. Byrd, who had aligned with Bacon against the Occaneechis, benefitted from the statutory changes that legalized Indian slavery in Virginia after the rebellion, and he enlarged the "market for the Indian slaves."‡ South Carolina's Lords Proprietors prohibited the enslavement of Indians, but Moore ignored them. He "let no one stand between himself and profits from the Indian trade" in slaves. Moore exploited the Westos for years before he led the fight against them. At the end of the seventeenth century he supplied weapons to the Waterees and "turned them loose on everyone else" to maintain a steady supply of slaves.§ The years between 1690 and 1715, La Vere argues, were "horror-filled years for the Indians of the American Southeast. No Indian town or village could count itself safe" from South Carolina's Indian raiders, who "would launch a surprise attack, gun down anyone who resisted, then capture everyone else." Gallay calculates that some thirty to fifty thousand Indians were "captured directly by the British, or by Native

---

* Traunter, *Travels*, preface, 7; Feeley, "Intercolonial Conflict and Cooperation," 70–71.

† Traunter boasted of this "new" road but provided few specific details about its route. By doing so, he maintained the confidentiality King William III required of him when the silver project was approved. Traunter gave specific markers for his 1698 journey on the main trade road, a route already familiar to traders in Virginia and the Carolinas.

‡ Ramsey, *Yamasee War*, 36; Gallay, *Indian Slave Trade*, 301; Rice, "Bacon's Rebellion," 749. See also Kelton, *Cherokee Medicine*, 41; J. L. Wright, *Only Land*, 135; Oberg, *Dominion and Civility*, 207; C. S. Everett, "They shalbe slaves for their lives," 87; Rice, *Tales from a Revolution*, 102.

§ Gallay, *Indian Slave Trade*, 93; La Vere, *Tuscarora War*, 52. See also Edgar, *South Carolina*, 98, 136.

INTRODUCTION

Americans for sale to the British, and enslaved."* The result was what Robbie Ethridge terms a "shatter zone" characterized by "widespread dislocation, migration, amalgamation, and, in some cases, extinction of Native peoples."†

There is no doubt that Traunter was involved in the Indian slave trade. When Byrd's traders carried their deerskins and furs to Traunter at the Appomattox store, they brought slaves as well. Moreover, Traunter's participation in the Indian slave trade is evident in his revenge motive for traveling, which was to answer an ambush on three South Carolina slave traders that occurred near the Roanoke River in 1697. Two of the men—Robert Stevens Jr. and John Hearn—worked for James Moore; the third man was Indian Jack, Moore's enslaved Indian.‡ After Jack appeared at the Appomattox store, Byrd reported that "an *English*man coming from South Carolina [was] murthered and robbed by Some unknown Indians." No action was taken by Virginia authorities.§ Hearn told South Carolina officials his assailants were ten Indian men: five Sugarees, two Keyauwees, and three Saxapahaws. Although South Carolinians wanted to prosecute the culprits, they had not bothered to cultivate alliances with upcountry Indians. The "price of their indifference" was that "Charleston had no sure means of contacting, much less coercing" Indians to assist them in making the perpetrators pay for Stevens's death.¶

The ambush occurred, according to Traunter, after Stevens, Hearn, Indian Jack, and some Wateree Indians—said to be Indian Jack's "Countrey men"—executed a slave raid against Occaneechis and Saxapahaws. In the course of

---

* La Vere, *Tuscarora War*, 52; Gallay, *Indian Slave Trade*, 299. Gallay indicates that South Carolina "exported more slaves than it imported before 1715" and that Indian slaves were exported to northern colonies, including Virginia, on ships (*Indian Slave Trade*, 299, 301–2).

† Ethridge, "Creating the Shatter Zone," 208. See also Hall, *Zamumo's Gifts*, 82.

‡ Robert Stevens Jr. was the son of Robert Stevens Sr., who, with five other members of James Moore's Goose Creek faction, "dominated the [South Carolina] assembly's affairs for a decade" (Sirmans, *Colonial South Carolina*, 70). John Hearn's family arrived in South Carolina in 1677. He owned a plantation on the west bank of South Carolina's Santee River (Webber, "Hyrne Family," 102; Ivers, *Torrent of Indians*, 87). Traunter's spelling for both men's names is inconsistent. In South Carolina records, only Stevens is used. In provincial records, Hearn is also spelled Herne.

§ Byrd I reported the incident to Governor Andros who issued an order on 25 October 1697 "to endeavor the discovery and apprehend or demand the mur-therers to be proceeded against" after two Indians questioned about the incident at Appomattox were "cleared" of blame then killed "the same evening by other Indians within our Settlements & habitations" (McIlwaine, *Journals of the House of Burgesses*, 105). See also copy of governor's address, 23 October 1697, in Palmer, *Calendar of Virginia State Papers*, 1:55.

¶ Salley, *JCHASC 1697*, 21; Merrell, *Indians' New World*, 51.

INTRODUCTION

the fight, several Occaneechis and Saxapahaws were killed; others were taken as "prisoners" to Carolina. Traunter implied that the three Charleston slave traders were transporting Occaneechi captives to Byrd in Virginia when, during the melee, the Occaneechis rescued their captured people with Tomahittan assistance.* Byrd and Traunter lost money as a result—in all likelihood far more than the £100 Traunter cited. It is telling that the ambush is the basis of Traunter's desire for revenge and the reason for his aggressiveness toward the Occaneechis. In spite of sharp objections by Byrd's more cautious traders, Traunter taunted the Occaneechis with Indian Jack during his 1698 visit to Occaneechi Town: he forced the Occaneechis to extend hospitality to Indian Jack, a man who had invaded their town and murdered their kin. In the midst of these tensions at Occaneechi Town, Traunter gave Eno Will a commission, what Will termed a *soc-ca-hick*.

Alliances that traders had with Native communities, and with individuals like Eno Will, often paved the way for productive intercultural negotiations. Traders acted as go-betweens who facilitated communication with Indians and colonists, a role that gave them considerable influence over Indian-English exchanges. At the same time, colonial officials worried that traders misused their connections and asked Indians to do their "dirty work," settling scores with other Indians or advancing personal agendas.† In 1714, for instance, South Carolina officials alleged that a trader named Alexander Long incited conflict between Cherokees and Yuchis with "a piece of paper disguised as an order from the governor" that encouraged Cherokee aggression against the Yuchis.‡ With Eno Will's *soc-ca-hick*, Traunter did something similar, even though Will's request for a *soc-ca-hick* seemed to catch Traunter

---

* Traunter alleged that the Occaneechis convinced a Tomahittan hunting party to undertake the ambush for a share of the spoils. The Tomahittans supposedly took the traders' guns, clothes, and money, then gave the Occaneechis their own deerskins in return. This distribution only makes sense if Tomahittans obtained captives as well. He also implied the Tomahittans were affiliated with the Iroquois. This is doubtful; Iroquoians considered the Occaneechis their enemies. Waselkov argues that the Tomahittans were probably a "Hitchiti-speaking group . . . that may have been a segment of the Tamas or Altahamas from southeastern Georgia" ("Seventeenth-Century Trade," 121, 118; Traunter, *Travels*, preface, 9–10, and Journal Two, 40–42). Needham and Arthur encountered Tomahittans in 1674 (Davis, "Travels of Needham and Arthur," 31).

† Merrell, *Indians' New World*, 74; Oatis, *Colonial Complex*, 23; Stern, "Economic Philosophies," 106.

‡ The dispute arose after a Yuchi man murdered a Cherokee (Stern, "Economic Philosophies," 103; Oatis, *Colonial Complex*, 101).

off-guard. Will dictated the terms to Traunter, who hastily prepared "the first thing that came into my head," a document using "a very large Character" that made it look official.* A council of Occaneechi "Great men" was convened during which Will announced that the *soc-ca-hick* made him "king" of the Occaneechis and allowed Traunter to "destroy Man Woman and Child of them" if they "offended" the English. With the *soc-ca-hick*, Traunter aimed to suppress Occaneechi resistance to colonial slave raiders, which he mischaracterized as making peace with them. The Occaneechis refused to legitimize the proclamation with gifts. They claimed to have "noe Deer Skins then in their Town" for Traunter or Will but said they would give them some at a later date. Later never happened. After Traunter left the town, the Occaneechis snatched the *soc-ca-hick* and evicted Will, which was why Will was living at Ajusher in 1699. A second *soc-ca-hick* was given to Will at Ajusher that licensed Indian aggressions against the Occaneechis, similar to what Long only allegedly did a few years later. It urged the "Shockoes, Acamantiaes, Enoes, Sapones, and Ajusheres" to seek assistance from the Tuscaroras "in killing the Occaneechees." The *soc-ca-hicks* were issued during Francis Nicholson's governorship, a time when, according to Rice, Virginians' "assaults against the neighbor Indians accelerated" but official repercussions were rare.† The coerciveness of the *soc-ca-hicks* was undoubtedly intensified by the fact that Traunter was Byrd's agent and known to Indians in the Southeast.

What bothered Traunter was the idea of Occaneechi power, perhaps even Occaneechi survival, since Ward and Davis estimate that fewer than seventy-five people lived at the Occaneechi village when Traunter was there in 1698.‡

---

* Traunter, *Travels*, Journal One, 23. Traunter emphasized his association with Eno Will and mentioned no alliances with Indian women. Unfortunately, as LeMaster points out, much less is known about "the significance of male-male friendships" ("War, Masculinity, and Alliances," 166, 173).

† Traunter, *Travels*, Journal One, 21, and Journal Two, 42; Rice, *Tales from a Revolution*, 215. The *soc-ca-hick* can be considered a form of inter-Indian diplomacy, an example of the "contacts, conflicts, and connections" among southeastern Indians that Richter and Merrell note are seldom evident in European accounts (preface to *Beyond the Covenant Chain*, xiv). The *soc-ca-hick* sheds light on another way Traunter may have empowered the Tuscaroras. On 2 May 1699 Nottoway Indians complained to Lt. Gov. Nicholson that Tuscaroras were "being incouraged" to purchase "Guns and Powder & shott" from the English at Appomattox which was used to overhunt game in Nottoway territory (Palmer, *Calendar of Virginia State Papers*, 65).

‡ Ward and Davis cite this population figure for Lawson's 1701 visit to the Occaneechis, so it should be a good measure of the Occaneechi community when Traunter was there in 1698 ("Tribes and Traders," 132). At the Fredericks site, Occaneechi Town at Hillsbor-

INTRODUCTION

The Occaneechis obtained tributary status under the Treaty of Middle Plantation in 1677; however, Stephen Feeley stresses that Virginia's tributary Indians were in a precarious position at the end of the century. They had "limited autonomy in many aspects of life and worried that Virginians would unilaterally abandon promises" to protect them against slave raids by southern tribes and Seneca marauders. The *soc-ca-hick* exploited those fears with insinuations of an intercolonial slaving coalition that did not exist, except possibly as a private enterprise between Moore and Byrd. While C. S. Everett alleges that Traunter orchestrated the Occaneechis' demise and paved "the way for a generation of traders," there is no evidence the *soc-ca-hick* had any material impact on the Occaneechis. Shortly after his excursions, Traunter disappeared from Indian-Anglo politics and from the historical record, so it is impossible to know what second act Traunter intended for himself. It is necessary, though, to distinguish between what motivated Traunter's ventures and why he wrote *Travels*. The reasons are not the same. Traunter's journeys fulfilled his obligation to find silver for William III. The "new" road meant that Indian slaves could be transported more surreptitiously between Virginia and South Carolina. The anti-Occaneechi rhetoric, however, that underpinned his narrative allowed Traunter to justify these motives, especially since he spilled considerable ink to recast events to present himself as an adventurer in North America's obscure regions.*

TRAUNTER'S AUDIENCES AND MOTIVATIONS FOR WRITING

The Travels of Richard Traunter was meant to entertain readers on both sides of the Atlantic while contributing to the body of natural knowledge about North America. Travel accounts about North America were immensely popular with seventeenth-century English readers because they "put the world on paper for the new print marketplace at home." These travelogues "inspired national pride" through an entertaining form of escapism that promoted economic investment in England's colonies as well.† One of the earliest writers to feed England's imaginative hunger for North America was Capt.

---

ough, archaeologists found "muskets and pistols, glass bottles and metal pipes, iron axes and pewter porringers" showing the Occaneechis "were thoroughly integrated into the colonial trade system" (Merrell, "This Western World," 23).

* Shefveland, *Anglo-Native Virginia*, 61; Feeley, "Intercolonial Conflict," 64; Everett, "They shalbe slaves," 92.

† Sherman, "Stirrings and Searchings," 19–20; P. Adams, *Travelers and Travel Liars*, 9.

INTRODUCTION

John Smith, who led readers through the marshes and mountains near the fledgling Jamestown colony and introduced audiences to Virginia's Native peoples in such works as *A Map of Virginia* (1612) and *The Generall Historie of Virginia, New-England and the Summer Isles* (1624).[*] In the decades that followed, travel narratives kept the English public informed about England's expanding imperial footprint. Edward Bland's *The Discovery of New Brittaine* (1651), *The Discoveries of John Lederer in three several Marches from Virginia, to the West of Carolina* (1672), and Thomas Ashe's "Carolina, or a Description of the Present State of that Country" (1682) took audiences ever deeper into today's states of Virginia, West Virginia, and North and South Carolina.[†] Second-hand accounts, too, had ready readers. Abraham Wood regaled Fellows of the Royal Society of London with the disastrous expedition of James Needham and Gabriel Arthur based on Arthur's testimony, a "flying report by some Indians," and details some Occaneechis gave to Henry Hatcher, a Virginia trader.[‡] The Royal Society of London, at the turn of the eighteenth century, not only functioned as "a clearinghouse for information" about distant regions, it also developed guidelines for natural history writing for use by "common seamen" and overland travelers such as Traunter.[§]

The Royal Society of London was founded in 1660 to promote Francis Bacon's "new science," which used inductive reasoning and methodical observation to ensure replicable findings.[¶] Society Fellows included scientific luminaries like Robert Boyle, Edmond Halley, Robert Hooke, and Isaac Newton, but most of its members were scientifically minded elites and politicians.[**] It

---

[*] Captain Smith parlayed his two-year tenure in Virginia into eight books about North America and his other travel exploits. Smith, *Map of Virginia*, in Quinn, *New American World*, 310–46; Smith, *Generall Historie of Virginia, New-England, and the Summer Isles*, in Horn, *Captain John Smith*, 199–670.

[†] Travel narratives were also a way to advertise the colonies. Salley notes that Ashe "designed" his pamphlet "to advertise the Lords Proprietors' real estate" (*Narratives of Early Carolina*, 137).

[‡] Wood did not write to the Royal Society directly. The details were conveyed in a letter written to John Richards (Davis, "Travels of Needham and Arthur," 36, 42–43). See also Needham and Arthur, "Journeys of Needham and Arthur," 215, 224–25.

[§] Parrish, *American Curiosity*, 65; Gascoigne, "Royal Society, Natural History," 546.

[¶] Gascoigne, "Royal Society, Natural History," 545, 546.

[**] Robert Boyle (1627–91) founded the field of chemistry with *The Sceptical Chymist* (1661). Edmond Halley (1656–1742) was an astronomer and mathematician who first predicted the orbital cycle of the comet known today as Halley's comet. Robert Hooke (1635–1703) conducted the first studies of microorganisms. Isaac Newton (1642–1727) was a mathematician whose laws of gravitation and motion, expressed in his *Principia Math-*

is not surprising, then, that the Royal Society's pursuit of natural knowledge was intimately tied to England's colonial agenda. Fellows reasoned that to "properly . . . possess new territories, one needed to catalogue their products and their peoples." Thomas Sprat articulated the society's conventions for natural history writing in *The History of the Royal-Society of London for the Improving of Natural Knowledge* (1667). Writers were advised to identify the "public utility" of natural resources with a "Mathematical plainness" that captured the "naked and uninterested Truth" of a subject without "amplifications, digressions, and swellings of style." These natural histories, according to Susan Parrish, "were descriptive prose catalogs of the flora, fauna, and often exotic human inhabitants of specific geographical places." Ideally, natural history transcripts avoided an "explanation of the causes which produced those phenomena" since, as society fellow Robert Boyle advised, a writer "should describe only what he knows from personal experience, so that the description of experimental 'facts' may be clearly demarcated from philosophical or theoretical 'opinions.'" The Royal Society encouraged travelers like Traunter to log their observations in order to provide its fellows with data to which they would not otherwise have access, thereby expanding the scope of natural knowledge.*

The intense demand for first-person reports about North America, Christopher Iannini explains, "provided one of the primary channels—in many cases, one of the only reliable channels—through which learned provincials could take part in the broader intellectual culture of the Atlantic world." Traunter's succinct natural history observations of the Southeast were consistent with the Royal Society's framework for objective reportage. Along his way he catalogued trees and shrubs, especially in riverine areas where fowl and fish congregated alongside commodities such as deer and beaver. The terrains—whether level, hilly, or dangerously rocky—were differentiated so traders had a "Usefull" map for future expeditions. Another component of *Travels* is what Angela Calcaterra terms "Indigenous content in [a] non-Native text."† The Southeast's Native peoples are central to Traunter's *Travels*. He focused on the location of Native towns and the "diplomatic" exchanges he conducted with Indians. Unlike Lawson and Byrd II, Traunter

---

ematica (1687), ushered in the modern era of science. Newton was president of the Royal Society from 1703 to 1727.

* Gascoigne, "Royal Society, Natural History," 539; Sprat, *History of the Royal-Society,* 26, 113; Parrish, *American Curiosity,* 18; Carey, "Compiling Nature's History," 292.

† Iannini, *Fatal Revolutions,* 4; Calcaterra, *Literary Indians,* 4, 8.

described no palisaded towns and rarely commented on the customs of the Indians with whom he stayed, perhaps because he was overly familiar with the people he visited.* However, when he witnessed something new, as he did with the burial of a six-year-old Waxhaw boy who died during the smallpox epidemic, Traunter recorded it with great care along with a discussion of the afterlife Indians anticipated for the child.†

It was often difficult for seventeenth-century readers to detect when travel writers strayed into fictional realms. Robert Beverley cautioned that "Travellers are of all Men, the most suspected of Insincerity." Even sincere travel writers recounted fabrications that had, as a result of repetition by respected men, acquired a scientific patina. An example from Virginia was the belief that rattlesnakes hypnotized their prey, particularly squirrels. Indians told Lederer that when rattlesnakes "lie basking in the sun," they "fetch down these squirrels from the tops of trees, by fixing their eyes steadfastly upon them" to the effect that the squirrels become mesmerized and tumble "down into the jaws of his enemy." Lederer thought the Indians were pulling his leg. Lawson conveyed the myth with less skepticism, noting that rattlesnakes "have the Power, or Art (I know not which to call it) to charm Squirrels, Hares, Partridges, or any such thing, in such a manner, that they run directly into their Mouths."‡ William Byrd II insisted that rattlesnakes "ogle the poor little animal till by force of charm he falls down stupefied and senseless on the ground." Naturalist Mark Catesby dismissed the phenomena, but Byrd doubled down and claimed that merely watching the process caused "a sickness at my stomach" due to the strength of the snake's charms.§ Beverley, too, depicted the snake's

---

* Lawson did much the same. By the end of his journey his descriptions are significantly foreshortened.

† Traunter, *Travels*, Journal One, 27–28. The Royal Society wanted travelers to inquire about Indian religious beliefs, mainly as a way to confirm "the biblical narrative" and affirm Christian dominance: see Gascoigne, "Royal Society," 542.

‡ Beverley, *History and Present State*, 7; Lederer, *Discoveries*, 145–46; Lawson, *New Voyage*, 134. The rattlesnake tale was published in the Royal Society's *Philosophical Transactions* with Paul Dudley's assurance that it was based on "many Witnesses, both *English* and *Indian*" ("Account of the Rattlesnake," 293).

§ Catesby wrote that it was "generally believed in America" that rattlesnakes charm their prey: "I never saw the Action, but a great many from whom I have had it related, all agree in the manner of the process" (*Natural History of Carolina*, 2:67). Byrd II claimed that the snake "moistens" the squirrel "with his spawl" to make it easier to swallow ("History of the Dividing Line," in *Prose Works*, 230; Byrd II, Letter to Catesby, in Tinling, *Correspondence*, 2:519). Byrd said also that bears must "sidle [down hills] lest their guts should come out of their mouths" ("Secret History of the Line," in *Prose Works*, 126).

INTRODUCTION

skill in his *History and Present State of Virginia* (1705). Traunter flirted with the legend when he disemboweled a rattlesnake and found a "whole Squirrell" in its "Belly," but went no further even though relating the process would have validated his authenticity with many readers.*

As a recorder of natural history, Traunter gives us descriptions of the Southeast's natural environment that remain compatible with twenty-first century science. But his was not a strictly scientific account. Scattered throughout *Travels* are humorous anecdotes about his own and his men's mishaps that were designed to entertain readers. In one episode, Traunter describes how one of his men, someone clearly not familiar with firearms, put "such an extravagant Charge" in his gun that the recoil "knock'd him downe" senseless. In another, Traunter's "Sword gott between [his] Leggs' and threw" him in the path of an enraged bear. There is also an adventure story embedded in Traunter's text. Nearly a quarter of Journal Two is an embellished rendering of the Occaneechis' retaliation against the South Carolina slave traders: the narrative trajectory portrays Traunter's expeditions as "soe dangerous an Enterprize" that Byrd's veteran traders refused to undertake it for fear of Occaneechi reprisals. It is more likely that Byrd's traders did not want to travel with Traunter if he intended to incite the Occaneechis to violence.† An odd aspect of Traunter's version of the Occaneechis' actions is the role played in it by Tomahittans. The only other appearance of Tomahittans in the seventeenth-century documentary record is Wood's retelling of Needham and Arthur's excursion that was sent to the Royal Society. It, too, recounted Occaneechi and Tomahittan violence, but it was not published until 1912.‡ Traunter's Occaneechi-Tomahittan tale features an example of what Richter says "came to be called

---

* Beverley, *History and Present State*, 239–40; Traunter, *Travels*, Journal Two, 43. Carey asserts that "in this era, wider parameters of belief existed not merely among the 'vulgar' but equally among educated and inquisitive individuals . . . in tandem with a certain readiness to embrace the monstrous" ("Compiling Nature's History," 290). Parrish discusses Cotton Mather's "Curiosa Americana," that "contained reports of mermen, two-headed snakes, and devouring (but at least buried) giants" (*American Curiosity*, 39).

† Traunter, *Travels*, Journal One, 14, Journal Two, 52, and preface, 7. Byrd I's traders went with Traunter to Occaneechi Town and continued to trade with the Occaneechis in ensuing years.

‡ The Needham and Arthur narrative was first published in 1912 by Alvord and Bidgood in *First Explorations of the Trans-Allegheny Region*. Traunter attributed the story to Eno Will, perhaps because in doing so he provided audiences with a "real" Indian story and had plausible deniability for its factuality (*Travels*, Journal Two, 40–42).

'Indian-style' fighting" characterized by "small-scale ambushes, [and] sharp shooting from protected locations." In Traunter's telling, five Tomahittans crept up on the sleeping traders, discharged a gun, then "imediately fell in with Clubbs." The sequence bears some resemblance to the Seneca attacks in Byrd II's "History of the Dividing Line." Byrd described how Senecas waited until their targets were "in a profound sleep" then "pour[ed] in a volley upon them.... The moment they have discharged their pieces they rush in with their tomahawks and make sure work of all that are disabled."* Richter attests to the historicity of such Seneca attacks, usually on their Siouan adversaries, but the basic elements also circulated in the region's folklore. As a growing number of Englishmen established themselves in the American colonies, stories about warring Indians proliferated in England and in North America, a good many of which perpetuated stereotypes that Indians were the antithesis of Englishmen and a threat to the colonial cause. In London, audiences would have read Traunter's *Travels* alongside a slew of recently published narratives about King William's War (1688–97) that showed colonists as victims of "fierce, formidable, furious, or terrible" Indians, including Cotton Mather's *Decennium Luctuosum: An History of... the Long War ... with the Indian Salvages* (1699).†

An account about a silver search in Carolina would have interested English and North American readers, but King William III's nondisclosure mandate prevented Traunter from writing that story. The fact that *Travels* has no direct references to the silver project, however, is evidence that the account was not written for an audience of one—Charles Montagu, to whom Traunter dedicated *Travels*—but for wider distribution. Montagu was privy to the project, so Traunter had no reason to withhold anything from him.‡ Instead, *Travels* gave flesh to political problems over which Montagu and the Board of Trade had jurisdictional authority. Traunter revealed how South Carolina threatened Virginia's economic stability—as well as Byrd's and his own profits— by interfering with trade conducted beyond its territorial boundaries. Vilification of Occaneechis invited more aggressive Indian policies by Virginia and London officials. Ultimately, though, by enumerating the region's wealth of

---

* Richter explains that this type of warfare evolved as Indians adapted to European technology (*Before the Revolution*, 140–41). Traunter, *Travels*, Journal Two, 41–42; Byrd II, "History of the Dividing Line," in *Prose Works*, 259.

† Berkhofer, *White Man's Indian*, 29; Barnett, *Ignoble Savage*, 5.

‡ In his capacity as Chancellor of the Exchequer, Montagu signed off on the initial funds given to the silver project partners.

natural resources, *Travels* advertised the economic opportunities that fueled English colonial expansion.*

THE TRAUNTER MANUSCRIPT

In his preface to *A New Voyage to Carolina* (1709), John Lawson complained that "most of our Travellers, who go to this vast Continent in America, are Persons of the meaner Sort, and generally of a very slender Education," who were "uncapable of giving any reasonable Account of what they met withal in those remote Parts." Lawson wrote to correct that deficiency. It appears that Traunter, too, attempted to address this "great Misfortune" with *The Travels of Richard Traunter*. Lawson's apothecary apprenticeship gave him an understanding of botany and natural science that contributed to his thorough assessment of the Southeast's plant and animal life.† Traunter's narrative is not as comprehensive as Lawson's, but it is not a rough assemblage of notes either. The information Traunter chose to include—and, perhaps more importantly, what he excluded—was intentional. Traunter made no mention of "trading girls" and referenced Indian women only twice: the Occaneechi women who offered him food and the Waxhaw women he startled in their remote village. It is difficult to read something into this omission because the only person Traunter described in depth was Eno Will.‡ It is just plain odd, though, that Traunter said nothing about trades in the Indian towns he visited, especially since he was a trader. He exchanged gifts and he underscored the need to observe hospitality protocols. He knew "there would be noe Travelling among [the Indians] if it were not for presents that we give them for their victuals." Still, only two gift exchanges were included in his journals—at Occaneechi Town and at the remote Waxhaw village. The Waxhaw incident is strange because Traunter supplied the "Gun, powder, shott[,] Salt, Beads, Duffill-Blanketts, and four yards of plaines" but had Eno Will deliver them. Also absent from *Travels* are any references to alcohol or drinking—by anyone in his party or by Indians—at a time when Lawson said rum was "so much

---

* In 1701 the South Carolina Commons House of Assembly passed a law that forbade Virginians and North Carolinians from trading with "South Carolina's" Indians, even when those transactions occurred outside the territorial boundaries of South Carolina (Cooper, *Statutes at Large*, 2:164–65).

† Lawson, *New Voyage*, 5; Lefler, introduction to *New Voyage*, xvi, xli.

‡ Lawson, *New Voyage*, 41; Traunter, *Travels*, Journal One, 20; Traunter, *Travels*, Journal Two, 49.

in Use with [Indians], that they will part with the dearest Thing they have, to purchase it." Traunter's companions, certainly Byrd's traders, carried alcohol for trade purposes since Virginia did not make it illegal to do so until 1705.*

There is a general absence of religiosity in Traunter's writing. Lawson thought every Christian man had a duty "to be serviceable in converting [Indians] to the Knowledge of the Gospel." Byrd II considered Christian conversion of Indians a necessary "civilizing" act and endorsed the separation of families by sending Indian children to the College of William and Mary "where they served as hostages for the good behavior of the rest and at the same time were themselves principled in the Christian religion."† Traunter rarely acknowledged God or Christianity, and he made no effort to convert the Indians. His dismissal of the Waxhaw afterlife, however, exposed an ideological blind spot when he lamented that "all the Heaven that those poor Indians expect" is that "they shall never dye again but hunt and glutt themselves as they did in this world." Traunter's depiction of the Indians' afterlife resembles what Lawson described as a "Country of Souls" where the dead "never meet with Hunger, Cold, or Fatigue." Byrd II called it a place where "spring is perpetual." Traunter's claim to be the first Christian on the new road between Virginia and Charleston indicates his concept of Christianity was less about faith and more in line with what Steven Oatis defines as an imperialist "desire to serve something greater than themselves," a notion predicated on "the superiority and political authority" of English culture and "the need to impose [English] economic and political authority on inferior parts of the world."‡

There are some discrepancies in Traunter's narrative. The Occaneechi treachery he foreshadowed at the start of Journal One never materialized. The alleged Occaneechi-Tomahittan conspiracy relayed in Journal Two happened before his own excursions took place. On his first trek it was Traunter himself who caused the "great deale of trouble" he had at an Indian town because his horses trampled Indian cornfields and destroyed "much" of the Indians' corn

---

* Traunter, *Travels,* Journal One, 20, and Journal Two, 50; Lawson, *New Voyage,* 18; Rountree, "Trouble Coming Southward," 77. Merrell explains that Indians "sought to treat alcohol as they did other foreign merchandise and make it fit existing cultural and ceremonial forms" until the destructiveness it unleashed made it impossible to do so ("Our Bond of Peace," 283).

† Lawson, *New Voyage,* 244; Byrd II, "History of the Dividing Line," in *Prose Works,* 220.

‡ Traunter, *Travels,* Journal One, 28; Lawson, *New Voyage,* 187; Byrd II, "Secret History of the Line," in *Prose Works,* 119; Oatis, *Colonial Complex,* 42. On Indian religion, see also Beverley, *History and Present State,* 154–70.

INTRODUCTION

"to their great losse." He justified the destruction by claiming that the road went "through their Corn fields." This makes no sense—and would not have made sense to those Indians either. An Indian road, which is what he was on, would have accommodated travelers without damage to corn crops. It would have been interesting to learn how Traunter reconciled himself with the rightfully angry Indians. The only tension with Indians Traunter recorded was at the remote Waxhaw village in 1699, when the women would not invite him into their community without Eno Will acting as chaperone. When Traunter neared the Waxhaw village, he "knew there could not be corne but there must be Indians," and this may be where he plowed through cornfields in his haste to find the "old" trade route. It would explain why Traunter gave so many trade goods to these Waxhaws and why Will delivered them instead of Traunter doing so himself. Traunter mentioned corn one other time, at the Suteree town, whose "very large feilds of Corn" were "at least Sixteen Miles long and almost as Broad." Despite their size, he presumably managed to steer clear of them as the Suterees "received [him] kindly" even though they were beset with smallpox and "very much dejected for the Loss of their friends and Relations."*

Most day-to-day aspects of life on the road were not included in Traunter's journals. It may well be that he underestimated readers' interest in the mundane aspects of his travels. Foods are mentioned in passing, usually just noting that his men "fared Sumptuously" when they had "both flesh and fish." Only one meal in an Indian town was described, at Occaneechi Town, where women gave him a dish of "Venison[,] Bears flesh boyld with Pumpkin" that did him "as much Good as any that I ever did eat in my life." The variety of that meal must have been a welcome relief from his near-daily diet of turkey. While Traunter wisecracked that "att length" the dogs refused to eat them, he took it in stride. In comparison, Lawson was "cloy'd with turkeys" before he reached the Congaree Indians early in his journey.† Traunter was amused when the Frenchman (probably Legaré, who was a silversmith by trade) wanted to know how to retrieve "the Blood that lay in the Belly of [a] Deer" so as "to make a pudding" from it. Traunter instructed him how to use "the Maw of the Deer and empty out the Excrement" to create "a pudding bagg."

---

* Traunter, *Travels,* preface, 2; Journal Two, 36, 49; Journal One, 28. The Indians and Traunter were probably responding to English colonists' long history of deliberately destroying Indian crops to compel submission and/or removal through starvation (Dunbar-Ortiz, *Indigenous Peoples' History,* 61).

† Traunter, *Travels,* Journal One, 17, 20, 25; Lawson, *New Voyage,* 33.

Legaré responded that "this [was] a right Soldier Shift" and thanked Traunter for his "Seasonable" advice. There was none of Lawson's reticence to eat fawns "boil'd in the same slimy Bags Nature had plac'd them in." Traunter groused because his men "left me ne're a Bitt" of the pudding. The "Millions of fleas" in "*Indian* Cabins" and the "huge Swarm of flies" in the wooded areas annoyed Lawson even though he traveled in the winter when insects were largely dormant. Traunter mentioned no insects, not even mosquitos, that thrive in the late summer/early autumn when he made his treks.*

Travels may have been drafted using field notes, as Traunter made simple dating errors. In the middle of the 1698 journal, he forgot to include non-travel days, a mistake perpetuated to the end of that report. The weekdays and dates in his 1699 journal are consistently out of sync by one day. An interesting aspect of *Travels* is that Traunter used two different calendar systems: 1698 was recorded in the Old Style, or Julian, format; 1699 was done according to the Gregorian New Style. New Style was not widely used during Traunter's time. Members of the Royal Society advocated for its adoption, but England did not officially implement it until 1752.† There are also mathematical irregularities in his mileage logs, some of which were deliberate. At first glance, the logs seem to support Traunter's assertion that the "new" road "cutt short [his] first journey by a very great many Miles": 941 total miles are listed for 1698 and 621 miles for 1699. His omission of 32 miles between the Congaree River and the Savana Hutts in 1699 was probably an honest addition error, the inclusion of which increased the total to 653 miles that year. Eyeing the mileage logs makes the 1699 trip seem about two-thirds of the distance recorded for 1698. The problem is that most traders going from Virginia to Charleston using the main trade road, without Traunter's deviations, would have traveled about 175 fewer miles than the 941 miles recorded on Traunter's log. Furthermore, Traunter stopped recording his mileage in 1699 at the Santee River, some 120 miles from Charleston, and sailed those last miles on James Moore's barge. To be fair, Traunter emphasized his travel "by Land" and the discrepancies were evident to anyone who scrutinized his figures and entries.‡

---

* Traunter, *Travels*, Journal Two, 45; Lawson, *New Voyage*, 58, 30.

† Content editing in the manuscript implies that Traunter wrote the manuscript himself, not a scribe, since most of the deletions and interlineations correct factual errors. See Cheney, *Handbook of Dates*, 11; Cheney, 1698 Old Style Calendar, table 34, 150–51; Cheney, 1699 New Style Calendar, table 29, 140–41.

‡ The actual mileage for Traunter's two trips is nearly identical. At least seven times in 1698 Traunter deviated from the main trade road and included those side trips in his mile-

INTRODUCTION

The *Travels* manuscript has the hallmarks of prepublication formatting. The title page, for example, has "The Travels of Richard Traunter" centered on four textual lines and written in a large, bolded italic display script (see fig. 1). Faintly ruled lines ensure the subtitle had a proportional formality that mimicked printed title pages. Traunter's dedication to Montagu makes it relatively easy to pinpoint when he completed *Travels*. Montagu is identified as Lord Halifax, a title William III bestowed on him on 13 December 1700. This means that the manuscript was completed after that date and before William's death on 8 March 1702, since Traunter also listed Montagu as "Auditor of *His* Majestys Exchequer."* If Traunter wanted "Travels" published, Montagu's endorsement would have been invaluable. Montagu was England's most generous literary and scientific patron. Recipients of his largesse included Isaac Newton (with whom Montagu had a lifelong friendship), the playwright William Congreve, John Dryden, Richard Steele, Joseph Addison, George Stepney, and Matthew Prior—the last two of whom served on the Board of Trade when Traunter presented his memorial in 1700. Unfortunately, Traunter could not have sought Montagu's patronage at a worse time. A partisan controversy caused Montagu to withdraw from public view at the end of William's reign until well into that of Queen Anne.†

Montagu's central role in London literary circles invites speculation about Traunter's publication aspirations, but it is plausible that Traunter had a more political agenda—to thank Montagu for his support of the silver project or to curry his favor. As an *ex officio* member of the Board of Trade, Montagu weighed in on Indian and colonial administration policies. The dedication to Montagu suggests that a copy of "The Travels of Richard Traunter" was presented to Montagu, since it was customary to provide dedicatees with such copies. It is even possible that the surviving manuscript was the one given to Montagu. Montagu's extensive collection of manuscripts, books, let-

---

age log. Most side trips were short, but each added at least 10 miles to his total. The most extensive deviation was about 73 miles traveled in South Carolina between the Wateree Indians and Hanging Rock east of the main Waxhaw Road. Deducting those miles puts his 1698 total at about 766 miles. Adding the 120 miles traveled by barge in 1699, and the mathematical error that omitted 32 miles, the total for 1699 is 773 miles (*Travels*, Journal Two, 36, 56, and Journal One, 34).

* Emphasis mine. Montagu retained his title as Lord Halifax after William's death but not the auditorship after Anne became queen. Traunter, *Travels*, dedication; Speck, "Religion, Politics, and Society," 49–59.

† Field, *Kit-Cat Club*, 7; Onnekink, "Anglo-French Negotiations," 167–68, 173–74.

xlvi

ters, and papers—including copies of Privy Council, Treasury, and Board of Trade proceedings—rivaled that of Sir Robert Cotton, whose holdings formed the basis of the British Library. After Montagu died, his library and art acquisitions were dispersed, initially to a nephew and to Catherine Barton, Isaac Newton's niece. More of Montagu's paintings and papers were sold in 1760. The auction catalog listed Montagu's artworks by artist and image, but his papers were advertised simply as a "collection of manuscripts . . . Relating to the manufactures, commerce, coin, colonies, public Revenues, public Accounts, and other public Affairs of the Kingdom of England in the Reigns of King William and Queen Anne," including papers about "Virginia, and various other Colonies in general."* It is also possible that the manuscript was given to John Smith, since an original Smith manuscript was appended to Traunter's "Travels." That seems unlikely, though. Smith undoubtedly kept copies of the affidavits he and his silver project partners submitted to the Board of Trade, but only the ones submitted in July 1700 were sold with "Travels," and Smith testified about the silver project at other times as well.

Auction purchases are confidential, which makes it difficult to reconstruct ownership of manuscripts like Traunter's, especially when transfers occurred centuries ago and/or between British entities. "Travels" was privately owned in England until March 1960, when Paul Mellon purchased it in an auction lot that included the four appended documents: seventeenth-century copies of "The Humble Memorial of Edward Loughton and Richard Tranter," "The Humble Memorial of John Smith," and a letter from Jean Couture. The fourth document is an original Smith manuscript, "An Abstract of the Proceedings relating to the Discovery of Silver Mines in Carolina."† *The Travels of Rich-*

---

* The disposition of Montagu's papers was not unique. The papers of John Locke and Isaac Newton were also consigned to disinterested heirs who sold, dispersed, and destroyed them. See Montagu, "To be sold by auction . . . a collection of manuscripts," 2, item 18. Montagu's vast art collection was auctioned earlier, in 1740 (Montagu, "Catalogue of the entire and valuable collection").

† To remove historical manuscripts from the United Kingdom, foreign purchasers must obtain an export license and provide microfilm copies of the manuscripts to the British Library; these copies are not included in the library's catalog. Traunter's "Travels" was sold by Christie's on 21 March 1960, lot 212 (Stansell, email, 31 May 2019). The shelfmark for the British Library's microfilmed copy of "Travels" is M/583. Had the four documents been purchased separately, they would have been independently microfilmed and shelfmarked. Three of the appended documents were seventeenth-century copies of records housed at the UK's National Archives, Kew, Surrey: Loughton and Tranter, Memorial, CO 5/1260/f.

INTRODUCTION

ard Traunter is essentially one artifact that contains two separately paginated day-by-day journals. The pages of "Travels" were sewn together in a manner that suggests it was done at the time the manuscript was written—and that both journals were written about the same time. The four silver project reports have matching crease-lines that indicate they were folded together before Mellon bound them into a single volume with Traunter's "Travels." In 2001 Mellon's estate donated the Traunter collection to the Virginia Museum of History and Culture in Richmond, where it has attracted the attention of scholars of history, literature, archaeology, and ethnohistory.*

What follows is an extraordinary opportunity to revisit the seventeenth-century Southeast through *The Travels of Richard Traunter*.

234–234v; Smith, Memorial, CO 5/1260/f. 232–232v; Couture, Letter, CO 5/1260/f. 236. The fourth appended item, Smith's abstract, appears to be an original document.

* The paper used for Traunter's journal is different than that of the copies. The page numbers for the Loughton and Traunter memorial, and Smith's memorial, are in the same seventeenth-century ink as "Travels." Smith's abstract and Couture's letter were numbered recently, in pencil.

THE TRAVELS OF RICHARD TRAUNTER

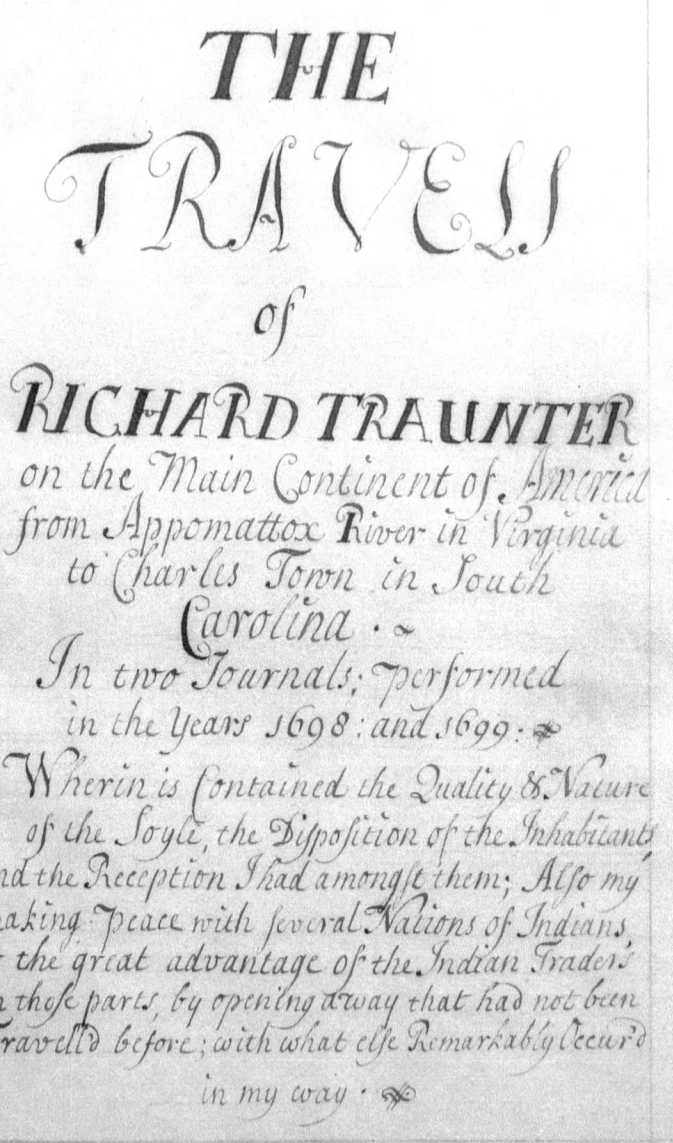

Figure 1. Title page, Traunter manuscript. (Virginia Museum of History and Culture, Mss5:9 T6945:1)

THE TRAVELS OF RICHARD TRAUNTER

on the Main Continent of America from Appomattox River in Virginia to Charles Town in South Carolina
In two Journals, performed in the years 1698 and 1699:
Wherin is Contained the Quality & Nature of the Soyle, the Disposition of the Inhabitants, and the Reception I had amongst them; Also my making peace with several Nations of Indians to the great advantage of the Indian Trader's in those parts, by opening a way that had not been Travell'd before; with what else Remarkably Occur'd in my way. [np]*

* Brackets indicate original manuscript's pagination; this page was unnumbered. A [P] marks the insertion of a paragraph break added for reading clarity.

TO

The Right Honourable Charles Lord Halifax,
one of the Lords of His Majestys most Honourable Privy Council,
and Auditor of His Majestys Exchequer,*
These Journals of my Travells in America are most humbly Dedicated,
intreating your Honour to Accept of this my poor Mite,
and to Pardon my unskillfullness in the performance,
most unfeignedly wishing your Honour all the Felicity this World can give,
and Eternal Happyness in that to come,
and humbly beg leave to subscribe
my self

Your Lordships
most humble & most
obedient Servant
Richard Traunter [np]

---

* Charles Montagu, Baron Halifax (1661–1715), was Auditor of the Exchequer in 1699. In 1698, as Chancellor of the Exchequer, Montagu signed the Treasury warrant that released funds to Traunter's partners in the Carolina silver project; he was also an *ex officio* member of the Board of Trade that approved the project (Speck, "Religion, Politics, and Society," 50; Treasury, William III to John Smith and Thomas Cutler, 515).

The Preface

[1] Before I proceed to my Journal, I thinke it requisite to give some Acco:t what were the Motives that induced me to undertake soe dangerous an Enterprize as this journey was esteemed to be in the Opinion of all but myself.

And they were chiefly Two.

The first was from a Naturall propensity I always had to travel; but more especially in untroden paths, thereby to discover the wonderfull workes of the Almighty brought forth by Nature, as-well to Enlighten the Intellect, as to gratifie the externall Senses; But my principal Aime and care was, to apply my Discoveries & Travels to the common Good of my Country, soe as to, make them Usefull to the Traders to those places I passed through, And to my power to render the Travelling to them more Safe than before had been, which I successfully performed by opening a free passage for Trade betweene *South Carolina & Virginia*, that never had any Comunication before by Land, I being the first man of his Majesties Subjects (or of any other Christian) that ever travelled quite through before, Though twice before attempted to noe purpose.[*] The first time they made [2] the attempt, they went from Carolina about halfe way, to a Nation of Indians called the Chyawey's[†] who told them

---

[*] At the time of Traunter's journeys, there was no routine traffic between the English settlements at present-day Richmond, Virginia (then called Appomattox), and Charleston, South Carolina. Virginia traders, including Traunter, regularly traveled from Appomattox to the Catawbas, near today's border between North and South Carolina, and went southwest from there to the Cherokees. But not south into Charleston. English colonists who lived in and around Charleston traded with Indians to the northwest and rarely ventured northeast. By 1700 more South Carolinians were traveling northward and engaging with upcountry Indians, as Lawson did when he went from Charleston to northern North Carolina in 1701. This may explain why Traunter claimed he was the first Englishman to travel the entire distance between the two colonial centers while also acknowledging Stevens's and Hearn's previously unsuccessful attempt to do so.

[†] Keyauwee Indians.

that if they went any farther, yt a Nation of the Indians called the Occaneeches would certainly kill them all, Soe they being afraid returned back again to Carolina.

The second Attempt was made in the year 1697 by one Robert Stevens, John Herne, and an Indian Servant of Captn James Moor's of Carolina called Indian Iacke, in which attempt Robert Stephens was murder'd by the Indians.[*] They were sent by Captn Moor from South Carolina,[†] with Intentions to buy horses in Virginia, and to bring them to Carolina by Land, they being very Scarce and dear in that Countrey & they being furnished with Horses, Amunition and Provisions for their journey, and One hundred pounds Sterling in money, They travelled Safe by the Assistance of Indian Iacke their Guide and Interpreter, till they pass'd the Occaneechee Towne and Ronoque River,[‡] and takeing up their Quarters that night on a small Neck of Land made by the River on one Side, and a litle Creek on the other, they thought themselves Secure; But in the Night when a sleep they were sett upon by the Occaneeches, as they believed, who shott Robert Stevens dead on the place, and shott the Indian through the Thigh. But John Herne leap'd into the River and Swamm over, and soe saved his Life, and whilst they [3] were rifleing of Stephens, the Indian though sorely wounded made his Escape and the best of his way towards Virginia which he reachd in Eleaven days to some of the Outsettlements on *Notoway* River, in a miserable Condition, not haveing any thing on him but a Blew Shirt, nor any thing to eat but what he could find on the Bushes all that time, haveing lost his Fire Armes. John Herne the next day accidentally meeting with some of the Indian Traders and telling them his, and his Companions misfortune, they went back to the place with him,

---

[*] Byrd I reported the incident to Virginia officials but did not identify any Indian suspects (McIlwaine, *Journals of the House of Burgesses of Virginia*, 105). On 12 November 1697, after John Hearn's return to Charleston, South Carolina's Commons House of Assembly alleged that five Sugaree, two Keyauwee, and three Saxapahaw men were responsible for the altercation (Salley, *JCHASC 1697*, 21). The man Traunter called Indian Jack, an Indian enslaved by Moore, may have been the same individual otherwise known as Wateree Jack, also held by Moore (Ivers, *Torrent of Indians*, 86–88, 118). Traunter variously spells Stevens's name as both Stevens and Stephens; see introduction, xxxiii*n*.

[†] James Moore Sr. (c. 1650–1706) was a leader of South Carolina's Goose Creek political faction and was heavily invested in the Indian slave trade. He served as governor of the colony from 1700 to 1703 (Oatis, *Colonial Complex*, 45).

[‡] Occaneechi Town was on the Eno River near present-day Hillsborough, North Carolina (Ward and Davis, "Introduction to Archaeology of the Occaneechi Indians," 2).

where he found their three horses and some of the money they had scattered in the dark, and the Corps of their friend Stevens sadly mangled, and his head bruised all to pieces; They sunk the Corps in the river & Herne return'd back to *Carolina* again not knowing but Indian Iack was killed alsoe, but he haveing received some small refreshments and makeing his Case knowne, was conducted farther into the Countrey to a house belonging to Colonel Bird of Virginia,* where I then lived and merchandized with the Indians for the said Colonel, who being acquainted with the miserable Condition of this poor Indian, he imediately sent for a surgeon. And in some time afterwards he was perfectly cured, and lived with me, and would often desire me to Enquire of the Colonel, when he would be pleased to send him home to his Master [4] in Carolina; I went to the Collonell and acquainted him that the Indian Slave was very desirous to goe again to Carolina. [P]

The Colonel told me that he should goe with the Traders when they came in, as farr on his journey as they traded, which was to a Nation of Indians called the Esaw's,† there being a Brother of this Indian that would conduct him safe to his master in Carolina; haveing told the Indian the Colonels intention to send him home, he was very well satisfied, att length the Traders comeing to the store that I lived att to pay in their skins and ffurrs, I asked them what News they could tell me concerning the murdering of Robert Stephens, and wounding the Slave; they replied, They could not tell, for some suspected it to be one Nation, and some another; The murders and the Contrivance of the murder not being discovered till my second journey to Carolina: This unfortunate accident proved my Second Motive to undertake this journey, to find out the murderers of Robert Stephens, and to revenge his Death on them, The Traders alsoe told me that the Wateree Indians the Slaves Countrey men had made Warr upon the Occhaneeche's and Suxabahaw's

---

* Col. William Byrd (1652–1704) of Henrico County, Virginia, was a prosperous Indian trader. He was a member of the Virginia House of Burgesses and Virginia Governor's Council; he served as auditor-general of Virginia until his death in 1704 (Tinling, *Correspondence of the Three William Byrds*, 1:3–4; J. L. Wright, *Only Land,* 69, 106–7; Briceland, *Westward from Virginia,* 4). John Hearn's last name is spelled in South Carolina records as both Herne and Hearn.

† The Esaws (or Catawbas) lived on the Catawba River on what is now the border between North and South Carolina (Merrell, *Indians' New World,* 92). In 1697 the South Carolina Commons House of Assembly ordered the Esaws "to Deliver up Those Indjns That Murthered Robert Stevens, into the Hands of this Governmt" to face murder charges even though there was no indication they were involved in the attack (Salley, *JCHASC 1697,* 21).

upon Suspition, killing some and takeing others Prisoners and carrieing them to Carolina.* On the other side the Occaneechees and Suxabahaws understanding that the Slave was in *Virginia* vow'd to take revenge on him or any one that should pretend to carry him home that way, which sorrowfull news I told the Indian, Neverthelesse he replied though the Traders were afraid of carrying him [5] home, he was not afraid to goe by himself, seing such Courage and resolution in the Indian, I told him that I would venture to conduct him to Carolina att which he seemed to be transported with joy that I that had been always so kind to him should even when every body else was afraid to goe with him, continue my care towards him and venture my Life through soe many Salvages that were in readyness to destroy Us, & Haveing with myself thus resolved to goe being (with an Ambition) animated to doe what none there dared to undertake but my self, I went and acquainted the Colonel that I had a great desire to goe upon such discoveries and attempts, alsoe to see *Carolina,* Att which he admired that I Should venture to goe, when the Traders themselves were afrayd of goeing; Not withstanding I was resolute and fix'd in my designe to goe, in defiance of all danger from the Indians, provided he could spare me from ye Store of Goods: When he saw my Resolution and that all his persuasions could not divert me from goeing, & he being very desirous that some body should conduct the [6] Indian back to *Carolina,* he assured me that I should neither want for good horses Arms Amunition and provision, and likewise advis'd me to be very circumspect in the Indian Towns least by Treachery they should kill me, which is always their Custom when they have Oportunity; for they dare not doe it openly. When the good Colonel had given me these and a great many such like Cautions, he wish'd me a prosperous journey which by the protection of Almighty God I very successfully effected, as I shall here relate, as alsoe the reception I mett with among those Indians that were, as the Traders told me in readiness to kill us, togeather with what was most remarkable in my journey.

Richard Traunter.

---

* Raids by Indians, such as this one in which Wateree raiders targeted the Occaneechis and Saxapahaws, procured slaves that were sold to English slave traders in South Carolina and Virginia (Gallay, *Indian Slave Trade,* 8–9).

JOURNAL ONE—1698
A Journal of my Travels from Appomatox River in Virginia, to Charles Town in South Carolina by Land.

[Traunter's 1698 journey followed the main trade routes through the southeast's piedmont. From Byrd I's Appomattox store Traunter took the Virginia Traders Path/Occaneechi Path to the Occaneechi Town at present-day Hillsborough, North Carolina. From there he traveled through today's North Carolina on the Esaw (or Catawba) Path until he reached the Suterees on what is now the border between North and South Carolina, at which point he turned due south on the Waxhaw Road that led into Charleston. This was the same route, in reverse, that John Lawson chronicled in 1701 from Charleston to Occaneechi Town.[*]]

[7] MUNDAY THE 15TH OF AUGST: 1698:[†]

My self & Company being well armed, horsed, and compleatly furnished with Amunition and provision, and all things necessary for Such an Undertakeing, and being likewise accompanied by four of the Virginia Traders, who had more courage than the rest, and would venture under my protection as farr as those Towns they traded to, Vowing they would stand by me to the last Gasp, w[ha]t with these Traders and my own men we were in all twelve,[‡] not

---

[*] Enduring names for rivers and many streams Traunter crossed indicate Englishmen were familiar with the main trade roads, including Lawson and Byrd II. The northern section of the route appears on the Fry-Jefferson map.

[†] Traunter used Old Style (Julian) dating in the 1698 journal (Cheney, *Handbook of Dates*, 150–51, table 34).

[‡] Traunter identified seven of the twelve men: Byrd's four traders, Indian Jack, Traunter himself and his servant. The other four probably were Edward Loughton, David Maybank, Solomon Legaré, and Henry Netherton, all of whom are mentioned in Loughton and Traunter's Memorial to the Board of Trade (appendix A in this work). There is also an unidentifiable person.

doubting but we were able to defend ourselves against a Nation of Indians, well knowing it to be their manner that if they see but a few men advance towards them with courage, not discovering any fear, they never stand battle, but make a Running fight of itt, and take some great Swamp or thickett of woods for their defense; But on the contrary if they discerne the least pusilaninity or [8] fear they will soon dispatch them, especially if they are hired by some other Nation; for they thinke it a very great Crime if they doe not performe their promise, in murdering those they are hired to kill, and believe they lose their honour & Reputation by not effecting their designe, they have once undertook to doe, for the furtherance of which, no possible Endeavors of theirs will be wanting, And 'tis too seldom they misse of their designe for either through carelessness, Or as I rather believe fear It has been the misfortune of Several Traders and others to fall into their mercyless hands, for certainly they are the most cruell, barbarous and Inhumane of Mortalls when in their power, as shall be related in its proper place.

Setting out from *Appomatox* in *Virginia* Wee travelled till we came to A place called *Monx-Neck-old-feilds** being about twenty Miles, poor and barren Lands but level, yet adorned with some Pine trees with shrubby Oaks and some Hiccary Trees† Lodging By a great Swamp of very thick woods and Bushes I sent out one of the men to hunt for Provision who returned a little before Night, bringing [9] with him two Turkeys which wee did Eat for Supper, and after wee had Sate a while and discoursed concerning the danger wee were to undergoe, and concludeing on the Methods for our preservation that night, wee went to Sleep.

TUESDAY AUG.ST THE 16TH 1698

In the Morning early Wee arose and haveing gott togeather our horses and pack'd our Baggage The Sun about an hour high wee sett forward on our journey, till haveing travell'd about twenty miles, the most part Hilly Ground and but indifferent Land, it being Oak & Hiccary Trees intermixt The sun being

---

* Traunter started his trek from Byrd I's store on the Appomattox River above the James River Falls in what is today Petersburg, Virginia. Monks Neck is "an English corruption" of "the old fields of Manks Nessoneicks" recorded by Edward Bland in 1650 (Briceland, *Westward from Virginia*, 44).

† Lawson said the ground nuts were mixed with venison broth (*New Voyage*, 35, 105). Beverley noted that Indians ground hickory nuts "in a Mortar with Water" to make a "White Liquor like Milk" (*History and Present State*, 142).

about an hour and a half high wee pitch'd our Camp att a place called the *Saponee Rocks** (being about twenty five miles from Monx-neck-old-fields) from whence we went a hunting. And haveing killed some Turkeys wee returned to our Camp and eat them, lying there that Night.

WEDNESDAY THE 17TH. [OF AUGUST]

Setting out abt Eight a clock in the morning from the Saponee Rocks, wee sett forwards on our way till wee came to a River called Nottoway river, being about Twenty Three Miles, for the most part Stony [10] hilly ground and most Oak and Hiccary, very few Pine trees; Upon the River [were] many Walls-trees with abundance of fruit, which river runs Eastwardly & empties itself into *Ronoque*-Sound.† This River abounds with abundance of very good ffish, On this River wee were forced to lye two days, by reason of much rain that fell: where on our arrivall wee killed Turkeys enough to Serve us that night, The next morning I took one of my men and went out a hunting to see if wee could kill any venison, for wee had not killed any yet; Wee hunted all that day and could not see any Deer; but discovered several places where ye Indians had been and sett Trapps to catch Beaver and Otter, the River much abounding with those amphibious animalls, togeather with Minx and Muck-ratts alias Mus-Guasts. My man putting me in mind to returne in time to our Quarters or Camp where the rest of our Company lay, Wee haveing for the most part of the day hunted upon the Level grounds off from the river. When steering to the River wee found it much farther than wee expected, When wee came to the River wee travel'd up the side thereof at least Tenn miles but discovered noe Camp,‡ and whilst Wee were considering whereabouts we were [11] and night approaching I concluded to lye there and in the morning

---

* Sappony Creek is in McKenney, Virginia. The Fry-Jefferson map shows the trade path near the rise of Sappony Creek. Sappony Church, or Chapel, built in 1725, was a road-mark for William Byrd II in 1733 (Byrd II, "Journey to the Land of Eden," in *Prose Works,* 410).

† Walnut trees. Roanoke Sound is now Albemarle Sound.

‡ This hunting trip was the first of several off-path excursions Traunter took during his 1698 journey. The distance put Traunter in the vicinity of today's Stony Creek, Virginia, near the "tuscaroora path" Henry Briggs referenced in a deposition to Philip Ludwell and Nathaniel Harrison around 1711. The "Tuscarora Road" went past what is now known as the Cactus Hill archaeological site, one of the oldest human habitation sites in North America ("Indians of Southern Virginia," 350; McAvoy, "Woodland and Historic Period Occupation," 279–80). Traunter's off-path treks increased the number of miles he traveled and recorded between Virginia and Charleston.

to find the Camp if possible & haveing sought a convenient place to rest our selves we laye downe, where not long after wee heard a Gunne goe off, but at a great distance from us as wee supposed by the noise, my man imagined it to be Indians that were a hunting and by reason we had hunted all the day & seen nothing worth killing thought, that they might have better successe, Notwithstanding I gott up and discharged my Gunn and ordered my man to doe the same, noe sooner had Wee discharged our Gunns but wee heard severall Gunns fire very soon one after the other,* says my man noto† The Indians know where we are they will come and kill us Therefore pray Sir Let us remove hence, I ask'd him where he would remove when 'twas soe dark that we could hardly see each other But instead of removeing I ordered him to load his Gunn againe when he swore he'd make them hear him and I discharged my Gunn alsoe But he haveing put such an extravagant Charge in his Gunn that when he discharged it, it knock'd him downe where he lay senselesse a considerable time When recovering I bid him goe to Sleep which he did, and a litle before day we gott up [12] and march'd along the River about five miles up, where we discovered our Camp four of our men being in readyness to come to See for us; But our Arrival prevented them who were very joyfull to see us returne safe for they were afrayd that wee had been lost, it being a very dismall thing to be lost in the woods, & being now very hungry our Company entertain'd us with both venison and Turkeys, haveing had better Luck than wee haveing made an end of my Breakfast which I ought to have had the day before, I returned God thankes for my good Chear and safe deliverance in not suffering me and my man to be longer Company for the Salvage Beasts, then I ordered the horses to be gott ready which accordingly were.

FRIDAY THE NINETEENTH OF AUGUST

We departing from this River, travell'd till about four of the Clock in the afternoon. It then raining very hard was the occasion of takeing our Lodging soe soon, whilst we were unpacking the horses it cleared up again, with that I ordered them to repacke those horses if they had unloaded which they did, Then we putt on againe and travell'd about five [13] miles where we arrived

---

* Traunter followed the English practice of firing guns in greeting or, in this case, to find the rest of his men; Lawson "charg'd [his] Piece" when he encountered English traders led by Massey on the trail (*New Voyage*, 60–61).

† "Noto" is a form of the Latin *notare*, meaning to mark or note, and was used to indicate dialogue.

upon a River called *Meherin-River* being about twenty Miles where we took our Lodgeings that night, where noe sooner we were settled but it began to rain and continued raining most part of that night, in the morning it begann to clear where we stay'd that day, it being Saturday for to dry our Goods, and in the mean time some of our Company went a hunting, and haveing killed a Deer and some Turkeys we continued there that night; The River being stor'd with all sorts of wild fowle, & abounding with ffish, alsoe with diverse species of Animals as Otter, Beaver, Musk-ratts, and Minx being of the amphibious kind Wee rested on Sunday, for I never did travel on that day.

MUNDAY THE 22D. [OF AUGUST]

Wee parted from Meherin River about Eight a clock in the morning, and travelling over good Land, being pleasantly deck'd with Oak and Hiccary, with abundance of Chink-Opien Bushes full of Fruit, Till wee came to a place called Rattlesnake Swamp, being about Twenty five miles: A Trader in the summer time travelling that way, had the misfortune to have one of his horses killed by the biteing of a Rattlesnake, from whence it's Name derived resting there that night.

[14] TUESDAY THE 23D. [OF AUGUST]

Wee Setting out about Seaven a Clock in the morning from Rattlesnake Swamp, & continueing our Journey till we came to a great River called *Ronoque* river,* being about Twenty three Miles, the Land covered with Oak & Hiccary with Chinck-Opem & Pine Trees. The River happened to be soe low that our horses foarded over without much difficulty, wee haveing a Canoe† for to transport our selves and goods being employ'd the best part of that day

---

* This is probably Moniseep Ford where Byrd II noted that "the Indian traders used to cross with their horses in their way to the Catawba Nation" ("History of the Divding Line," in *Prose Works,* 230). The trade road that crossed the Roanoke River at Moniseep Ford went to the Occaneechis' new town at Hillsborough (Davis, "Cultural Landscape," 152).

† Traunter carried "a canoe," but he may have also used canoes that Indians stashed at waterways for general usage. According to Ethridge, ethnographic evidence indicates that "Indians kept a plentiful supply of canoes on hand for river crossings and transport" and "hid canoes in plain sight at river crossings by keeping the bark on the underside of the canoe and turning it over so it looked like an old log" ("Navigating the Mississippian World," 71).

in getting over our Goods and horses, & was forced to stay there On Wednesday for to find two of our horses that were missing; On this River in the Season of the year may be seen such inumerable flocks of Swans wild Geese Ducks of all sorts. The Land of each Side haveing Ponds or Lakes that are also stock'd with Ducks in such great quantities that if a stranger should see them especially when they are disturbed and take Wing he'd certainly conclude that all the Ducks on the Continent were gathered together on that River, and Ponds, round about which are very Spacious Savanaes or Meadows intermix'd in divers places with most pleasant Groves so plentifully [15] abounding with such variety of medicinall herbs that if ever *Æsculapius'* had his residence in the American parts, I Should verily have believed that place to have been his Garden. Alsoe the adjacent woods are well stock'd with Deer, Bear, Tiger[†] and Wolf, Fox, Catt Raccoan, Monack[‡] and Opassum, with a great many more of the Salvage kind too tedious here to name. Upon this River Ronoque there grows a Tree or Shrubb, which if a piece of the wood of it be taken in ones hand it is of soe Venene[§] a quality that the partie touch'd with it immediately dies, Also any manner of Edge-Tools that cutts of it and afterwards cutteth meat, Notwithstanding the meat being boyld or roasted after the Knife or Axe hath cutt it, the partie that eats of the meat will unavoidably dye without Remedy, itt haveing such Speedy Efficacy Some Englishmen Seeing the Effects of it did verily believe it to be the Strongest poyson in the world, haveing given this brieffe account of this River I shall proceed.

THURSDAY THE 25TH. [OF AUGUST]

Setting out about [16] Nine a Clock in the morning Wee travel'd from Ronoque River to a place called the hazle swamp,[¶] being about Twenty five Miles, Where wee were noe sooner arrived but our Company soon employ'd

---

* Aesculapius was the Roman god of medicine and healing.

† The eastern cougar was also known as a deer tiger. Byrd II says that "in South Carolina they call this beast a tiger, though improperly" ("History of the Dividing Line," in *Prose Works*, 255).

‡ Monax was an indigenous word for groundhog or woodchuck (*marmota monax monax*) (Hodge, *Handbook of the American Indians North of Mexico*, 940).

§ Venomous. Lawson described a "poison vine," the juice of which caused stains that could not be washed out (*New Voyage*, 107).

¶ Traunter's mileages suggest that Hazel Swamp was not on the main path. This may be Nutbush Creek that was so named because of "the many hazel trees growing upon it" (Byrd II, "History of the Dividing Line," in *Prose Works*, 232).

themselves in gathering Hazle-nutts, This place plentifully abounding with them from whence it was called the Hazle Swamp, where wee lay that night meeting with nothing matteriall in this days journey.

FRIDAY THE 26TH. [OF AUGUST]

Wee sett out from Hazle Swamp, and travel'd untill wee came to A place called Hatcher's Run* being about twenty five Miles where we lay that night, In the morning one of my men goeing out to look my horses and missing one of them, he rambled soe farre to find him that he lost himselfe, which caused us to stay there Saturday for to find him, I sent out three of our Men Three several ways but they all returned without the man; then I imagined he was lost for certaine. Nevertheless I ordered every man to load his Gunn and Stand in a line bifore me, and giveing the signall they all discharged together which made a Report like a great Gunn; I my self fired a pistoll in Each hand and haveing ordered them to load againe wee all discharged as at first, and not long after wee heard a Gunn but att a great distance, with that wee continued Charging & discharging till by the report of our Guns my man was directed to the Camp, but it being late in the Evening wee did not sett out that day.

[17] SUNDAY THE 28TH. [OF AUGUST]

Wee sett out from Hatchers Runn, it raining soe very hard that wee were enforced to depart thence, there being noe shelter for us, Otherwise I should not have travell'd on this day and journeying to a place called the *Napp of Reeds*† it continued raineing soe very hard that wee were forced to use our uttmost Endeavour with difficulty to make a fire which is the first thing wee doe when we come to a place for to lodge, some of my men goeing out a hunting returned and brought with them some Turkeys, haveing employ'd myself and one of my men in catching fish, there being a Creek that plentifully abounded with a sort of fish call'd a ffattbacke, also with Pike and Roche, wee fared Sumptuously in this place haveing both flesh and ffish.

* Hatcher's Run is north of present-day Durham, North Carolina.

† Knap of Reeds Creek is north of Durham. Myer notes that there was an "ancient village on Knap of Reeds Creek, near the modern village of that name, in Granville County, N.C.," but that village seems to have been subsumed by Dutchville and Butner ("Indian Trails of the Southeast," 776).

MUNDAY THE 29TH. [OF AUGUST]

Setting out about Eight of the Clocke in the morning and Crossing the Geniton-Tarr River* wee came to a place called the Enoe-feilds,† where there are very large fields with abundance of Peach Trees, and Mulberry & Some Chesnutts, there being very rich Lands and abundance of it;‡ Formerly a Nation of Indians called the Enoes inhabited this place They were driven from here by the *Tusk-Aurora*§ Indians then destroying a great many of them, and other Nations Since, So that there are but very few left, those now liveing have joyned themselves to a Nation of Indians called the *Shockoes.*

TUESDAY THE 30TH. [OF AUGUST]

Wee sett out from the Enoe fields, and travell'd till wee came to a place called the Occaneechee Creek,¶ where haveing killed [18] some Turkeys we stayd there that night; In this days journey I saw severall great heaps of stones wch the Indians had cast up togeather, They signifieing by those heaps of Stones that formerly there had happened a very great fight in this place, Where severall great men of the Indians were slaine and in memory thereof whenever they goe to this place The Indians always cast a stone to the heap, that if there goe never so many by they are bound to cast each man a Stone and noe more.**

---

* There is no Geniton-Tar River. Three rivers in the area are Flat River, Little River, and Eno River.

† Archaeologists identified evidence of seventeenth-century Eno villages in the upper Neuse drainage and in the Eno–Flat River drainage (Davis, "Cultural Landscape," 152–53; see also Davis and Ward, "Evolution of Siouan Communities," 43–44, 52). This may be the Shakori village visited by Lederer, now the Jenrette site near Hillsborough (Beck, *Chiefdoms, Collapse*, 172).

‡ Hammett notes that "tree crops," like those described here, were generally associated with Old Fields ("Ethnohistory of Aboriginal Landscapes," 34). Peaches, introduced by the Spanish, were cultivated by Indians and considered a "native" crop by 1700 (Merrell, *Indians' New World*, 16).

§ The Tuscarora are an Iroquoian people who lived in eastern North Carolina between the Roanoke and Neuse Rivers (La Vere, *Tuscarora War*, 43).

¶ In 1699 Traunter identified Occaneechee Creek as Doe Swamp.

** Lawson observed a similar practice between the Catawba town and the Saponis (*New Voyage*, 50). Lederer mentioned "a pyramid of stones" that "was the number of an Indian colony drawn out by lot from a neighbour-countrey over-peopled, and led hither by one Monack," or Monacan (*Discoveries*, 149).

JOURNAL ONE—1698

WEDNESDAY THE 31TH. [OF AUGUST]

This morning bifore wee sitt forward on our journey I took particular care that my men put flints in their Gunn locks, and pistolls alsoe, ordering them how to encounter the Occaneeches if in case they gave us battle, Wee being then within Twenty Miles of their Towne; For it is to be remembered that they vowed to kill the Indian that I then was carrieing to Carolina, or any one that Should pretend to protect him, which I was resolved to doe or lose my life haveing thus put my Self and Company in a posture of Defense, Wee marched untill wee came to a small Hill which was within Muskitts-Shott of the Towne* as soon as wee were arrived Wee discharged severall Pistolls, which is a Custome that the English always use when they come to an Indian Town,† Hearing the noise of our Arms a great many of the Indians that were in the Town came running up the Hill towards us, And as soon as they were in Sight I putt Spurs to my horse and boldly [19] mett them, They tooke me by the hand and askd me how I did, I answered and told them in the Tuskauroran Language which I well understood,‡ That I had brought the Indian Slave that they said they'd kill or any one that should Speake in his defense, and withall I told them that if they were for fighting and performing their promise, I was there to defend the Indian and to give them Battaile fairly which was soe farre from their fashion of fighting that they told me they did not know me, and that they had noe quarrell agst the Indian, desireing me to unpacke my horses and lye in their Town that night, But I refused to lye in their Town and Encamp'd on the Hill. [P]

I made them and the Indian I had shew friendshipp and greet each other after the Indian Manner, which they Accordingly did by stroakeing Each other

---

* Occaneechi Town on the Eno River east of present-day Hillsborough, North Carolina, is now the Fredericks archaeological site (Davis, "Cultural Landscape," 152; Ward and Davis, "Introduction to Archaeology," 2; Beck, *Chiefdoms, Collapse*, 172; Dickens, Ward, and Davis, introduction to *Siouan Project*, 1–2).

† Lederer said travelers "must give notice of your approach by a gun" at some Indian towns, but not all, since Indians not accustomed to the shots fired "would affright and dispose them to some treacherous practice against you" (*Discoveries*, 169). Beverley added that "Strangers" are met "by a great Retinue" about a "quarter or half a mile" out of the town where the "Ceremony of the Pipe" and other hospitality rituals were conducted before visitors were invited into the community (*History and Present State*, 148–49).

‡ The Tuscarora language had become the "Indian lingua franca" in eastern North Carolina (La Vere, *Tuscarora War*, 47).

down the Arm It being the Custome of most Indians in those parts,* which being accomplish'd the Indians all departed to their Towne, And I could not forbear laughing att the Traders, and told them that I hoped that they were now Sensible how Indians might be managed, provided a man be not afrayd of them; Wee had not been there half an hour but the Indian women were sent with Severall Bowles of victuals to us, which they presented to me, and the Traders that were with me; It being a Token of great Friendshipp Notwithstanding some of our company desired me that I would not eat of the Victualls least there should be poison in it, However I did eat and when they Saw [20] me eat They did eat of it alsoe, And I thought the victualls did me as much Good as any that I ever did eat in my life, there being Venison Bears flesh boyld with Pumpkin wch was instead of Bread For which I gave unto the Indians some Tobacco some Beads powder Shott Salt and severall other things, a little of most things wee had. There would be noe Travelling among them if it were not for presents that we give them for their victuals, For they expect that one should present them considerably. [P]

After all these Ceremonies past between us and the Indians They invited me down to their Town, and alsoe the Indian that was with me, which I thought did not sound very well, by reason they invited none of the Traders, Neverthelesse I was resolved to goe & See their Town and withall I told the rest of my company That if I did not returne or Send to them in halfe an hour They might reasonably believe the Indians had dispatch'd me, And the Indian I had with me, haveing my Gunn Pistolls and Sword The Indian alsoe haveing his, Wee walk'd down to their Towne Two of their Grandees walking before us, where being arrived one of the great men entreated me to walke into his house He went in before me and I followed him, where there was a Matt upon a Hurdle when he bid me Sitt downe Then I sate down and he sate by me, Then I enquired of him where an Indian was, called Enoe Will,† Who told me that he and [21] Tenn Indians more were a hunting, I desired him imediately to send an Indian Runner for him and also his company; This Enoe Will being a very good Friend to the Traders when they used to trade

---

* Lawson mentioned a similar act whereby "the Man of the house scratch'd this War-Captain on the Shoulder, which is look'd upon as a very great Compliment among" Indians (*New Voyage*, 48).

† In 1701 Lawson met Eno Will at Occaneechi Town, then Will took Lawson to Ajusher (*New Voyage*, 61).

there, I my Self was very well Acquainted with him and durst trust my life in his hands thô in none else in the Towne, When he was come after he and his company had putt up their Meat, He and they came to me and presented me with as much Bear and Venison as I could well carry; But when he perceived 'twas me, he wonder'd I should bring the Indian For he told me his Townsmen did Say they would kill the Indian; But he told me that since I had brought him I need not fear Them, and that they would not offer any Such thing, But he did believe had the Traders brought him the Indians would have kill'd him; And withall earnestly desired me to give him a Commission to be King of these Occhaneechees, in his Language calling the Commission a Soc-ca-hick Haveing assembled all the great men and those that were the Warriours, he took me into his house, And I told him I had a Soc-ca-hick for him provided he would promise me upon honour That he would Ayd and assist the Traders, and See that the Indians did them noe wrong whenever they should come there to trade, [P]

These and a great many Such like promises he faithfully promised me he would performe By virtue of the Soc-ca-hick then he called all the Great men of the Town and the Warriours and having they after their manner called a Councill, He desired me to Sitt down, togeather with all my Company one Side [22] of the house and the Indians on the other Side, there being a fire between us, Enoe Will placeing himself just by me He took the Soc-ca-hick in his hand and told them what they must trust to if ever they offended the English, That I would certainly come and destroy Man Woman and Child of them, and not leave them one house standing in their Town, To which they replyed they would be very good to the English, Then he told them that the Soc-ca-hick then in his hand was Given him by me to make him their King, Then one of the great men asked me in the Tusk-Aurora Language whether I sayd it should be Soe that he Should be their King by Virtue of the Soc-ca-hick or not, To which I replyed That he Should be their King, And that wch he Should Say to them, Should be a Law, When they perceived I had made him their King They seem'd well pleased, and told me They had noe Deer Skins then in their Town either to present me with or their New king, But they told me they would have a good Present for me of Both Skins and Furrs when I return'd from Carolina.

Haveing thus treated with my enemies and staying there Thursday and Friday to make an end of this State Affaire the New King entreated me that he and his men might attend me to the next Indian Town which was called the Chyawey's, to the end they might See his Soc-ca-hick And that he might engage them alsoe to be kind to the English.

SATURDAY THE 2D OF SEPTEMBER*

We sett out about Tenn of the Clocke in the morning The Indian King takeing no small paines to Spruce and paint himself which they always doe when they have a journey to goe, Haveing taken our leave of the Indians we travell'd till we came to a River called the Haw River† where we lay that Night. The Indian [23] King and his man went a hunting for us but return'd without any thing for us. We lay there Sunday.

MUNDAY THE 4TH. [OF SEPTEMBER]

We sett out from the Haw River and came to a place called the Fish Swamp where we lay that night the Indian King sent his Man out a hunting who killed a large Doe I and my Indian went a fishing and haveing catch'd some fatt-Backs we returned to our Camp where we employ'd our Cooks some with Venison some with Fish fareing Sumptuously that night.

TUESDAY THE 5TH. [OF SEPTEMBER]

We sett out from the Fish Swamp till we came to a River called the Diep River,‡ But about three Miles before we came to the River one of my men was goeing before the horses and another behind The hindmost calling out to the foremost, who looking about saw Three Deer that Ran between him and the horses, And two that ran among the horses He fired among them and killed a stately barren Doe that was very fatt, and alsoe wounded one of my horses that when I came to Search him I found Three Swan-shott, one in his Briskett The other two in each of his fore-leggs, One I found not out till I came to the River where we lay that Night.

---

* Saturday was 3 September in 1698, Old Style calendar. The date-weekday dating error is continued until 27 September.

† Haw River intersected with the trade road at Swepsonville, North Carolina (Rights, "Trading Path," 406). See also Troxler, "Places and People," 28; Fecher, "Trading Path and North Carolina," 8, 9.

‡ The Trade Path crossed the Deep River near Randleman, North Carolina (Rights, "Trading Path," 406; Rights, *American Indian in North Carolina*, 85).

JOURNAL ONE—1698

WEDNESDAY THE 6TH. [OF SEPTEMBER]

We sett out from Diep River and travelled untill we came to the Chyawey's Town,* The Indians received us kindly And our Indian King assembled the Chieff men of the Towne and shew'd them the Soc-ca-hicke that I had given him att the Occaneechee Towne Which when the Chyawey's understood They respected me as though I had been King my selfe, Then I told them as I had done att the other [24] Town that they must be kind to the Traders, and Suffer Carolina Men to come that way to Virginia and the Virginians to travell safe to Carolina, which with a mutuall Consent they promised me they would, There being the Saxa-ba-haws† there at that time, soe that I made peace wth Three Nations (viz.) The Occaneechees Chyawey's and the Saxa-ba-haw's, who all respected the New King more than all the other Kings in those parts of the World, merely through a fear they had to his Soc-ca-hick or Commission, For I scarce believe that ever an Indian King before was instituted by an English Commission. The Commission being only what first came into my Thought, and written in a very large Character, The letters att least an Inch long, which made it looke great. The Nations alsoe of the Shockoes, Acamantiaes‡ Enoes Sapones and Ajusheres highly respected this King: The Virginia Traders alsoe assureing me that they never Traded So peaceably in their lives as they have done since this King had his Commission. Thus Enoe Will who dwelt with the Occaneechees ruled and bore as much Sway in his Dominion, and was altogether as absolute as the Great Mogull,§ The Indians in generall

---

* Keyauwee Town was on Caraway Creek west of present-day Asheboro, North Carolina. It is now the Poole archaeology site (Davis, "Cultural Landscape," 135, 150; Beck, *Chiefdoms, Collapse*, 52).

† Saxapahaw or Sissipahaw Indians.

‡ Shakori and Acamantiae Indians, which Traunter identifies as distinct peoples. The name Acamantiaes may be a phonetic variation of Aramanchee or Aramancy. The Aramanchee River, also spelled Aramancy and Aramanchy, appears on colonial maps (Popple, *Map of the British Empire*; Fry and Jefferson, *Map of . . . Virginia*). Aramanchy River is now called Great Alamance Creek.

§ Eno and Saponi Indians. Traunter suggested the Ajusher Indians had a unique identity and were not simply residents of Ajusher. The diversity of people living at Ajusher indicates that it was a coalescent community which was formed of "people from different cultures, societies, and languages" (Ethridge and Hudson, qtd. in Beck, *Chiefdoms, Collapse*, 7; Davis and Ward, "Evolution of Siouan Communities," 52). The "Great Mogull" Traunter referenced was Emperor Aurangzeb, the sixth Mughal emperor of India. He declared war against the English East India Company in 1695 after Captain Every, an English pirate, captured his vessel carrying pilgrims to Mecca, terrorized the passengers, and raped

imagining That there was Something extraordinary in the piece of Paper, Enoe Will being not a litle proud of it himself.

THURSDAY THE 7TH. [OF SEPTEMBER]

This morning wee departed from the Chyawey Towne and Enoe Will travell'd [25] with us about Three miles to the foot of a great Rocky Hill where he and I parted, discovering to each other great friendship & Haveing thus taken leave of the King I directed my Course up the Hill, It being Soe rocky that the horse my man had wounded when he killed the barren Doe broke both his Fore-leggs, just in the places where the Shott enter'd, Soe that it was impossible that he Should live or be able to move out of the place. I ordered one of my men to Shoot him Then I putt forward again, till I compass'd the Topp of the Hill and continueing on our way till we arrived att a place called the Haw Swamp where wee Encamped that Night.

FRIDAY THE 8TH. [OF SEPTEMBER]

We Sett out from the Haw Swamp and travell'd till we came to a place called *Whettstone Creek*,* where we went out a hunting and kill'd Some Turkeys In this days journey I had a horse tired that I was forced to leave behind.

SATURDAY THE 9TH. [OF SEPTEMBER]

We sett out from Whettstone Creeke, and travelling till we came to a very fine River called *Yadkin*, alias—Cape fear River,† There being a most pleasant Is-land (in this River) which we went through in crossing the River. Being come to the other side our men killed some Turkeys, This River plentifully abound-ing with very good Fish of severall sorts Also Beaver, Otter Minx, and [26] Muskratts In Winter it soe plentifully abounds with wild Geese, That when

---

several of the women (Hanna, "Protecting the Rights," 303–4; Nutting, "Madagascar Con-nection," 205).

 * Probably the Uwharrie River, where Lawson too noted the abundance of "hones" (*New Voyage*, 56). Daniel and Butler found ancient quarries in this area ("Archaeological Survey and Petrographic Description," 25–26, 34).

 † Traunter misidentified this river as the "Yadkin alias Cape fear River." Yadkin River becomes the Pee Dee River. The trade road forded the Yadkin River north of Spencer, North Carolina, at a location known as Trading Ford or Yadkin Ford.

the Traders have been there They have killed such Quantities of them That att length their Doggs have refused to eat them, Wee continued here Sunday.

MUNDAY YE 11TH. [OF SEPTEMBER]

We Sett out from Yadkin River, and continued our way till we came to a place called the *Licking Branch,* where there is a Clay Bank that the Deer always come to lick att And they have soe lick'd away the Bank in severall places, and thereby made it hollow, that it seems like soe many severall Cellars or Vaults. The reason the Deer come here to lick more than any other place is, because the Earth tastes somewhat Salt, There being Severall of these places in my Journey.

TUESDAY THE 12TH. [OF SEPTEMBER]

We sett out from Licking Branch, and travell'd till we came to a place called the Crosse paths,* when goeing out a hunting I happen'd to come to a place where there were abundance of Hazle Nutts, And not farre from the place where I gather'd the Nutts there were abundance of Vines with inumerable Clusters of Grapes full ripe, And whilst I was gathering the Grapes I was like to tread upon a Rattle Snake which If I had, it would undoubtedly have kill'd me by its biteing, But I perceived it as I was just goeing to tread upon it and Shott it. It had Seaventeen Rattles in its Tayle being a very [27] large Snake, and Seaventeene years old according to the Number of Rattles, One yearly being added to their Tayle.

WEDNESDAY THE 13TH. [OF SEPTEMBER]

We sett out from Crosse paths and travell'd till we came to a place call'd the Great Creek, being very plentifull with Severall sorts of good Fish.

---

   * Two main intersections, or cross paths, were on the trade road south of Yadkin Ford: one at Salisbury and another farther south between Harrisburg and Concord that forked again at Steele Creek in present-day Charlotte, North Carolina. From the Harrisburg/Concord cross, one path went to the Suterees while another arced west then south toward the Esaws (Rights, "Trading Path," 405; Fecher, "Trading Path," 8; Collet, *Compleat Map of North Carolina*). It took Traunter two days to get from the Yadkin River ford to the cross paths, which suggests he was at the Harrisburg/Concord cross. He did not indicate when Byrd's traders left his party, but they were headed to the Esaws and Traunter to the Suterees.

THURSDAY THE 14TH. [OF SEPTEMBER]

Wee sett out from the Great Creek; and travell'd till we came to *Triangle Creek,* where we went out a hunting and killed some Turkeys We lay there that Night.

FRIDAY THE 15TH. [OF SEPTEMBER]

We Sett out from Triangle Creek and travell'd till we came to a Nation of Indians called the Suterees,* These Indians received me kindly though att that time they were very much dejected for the Loss of their friends and Relations, The Small Pox† haveing been brought amongst them which Distemper they never knew before, and was the Cause of their mortallity and hardly a person in the Nation escaped this Distemper, whereof Some hundred dyed; It being the worst of Distempers that could befall the Indians For their Manner is, when ever any sickness happens to an Indian He imediately by the advice of the Indian Doctor goes into the Sweating house which is a place that has no vent, but the Door they go in att like an Oven with a great heat in it which is very hott and Stiffling, And comeing out of the Sweating house in that very instant he jumps into a pond or River, though it be in winter time which they generally hold as a [28] great means of their Recovery; But in the Small Pox their Method had a quite contrary Effect, For noe Sooner came they out of the Sweating-house and jump'd into the Water, but they dyed in few hours after.‡ About this Indian Town There were very large feilds of Corn being at

---

* Suteree was an alternate spelling for the Sitteree Indians, who lived near the Sugarees on Sugar Creek in what is now York County, South Carolina (Beck, *Chiefdoms, Collapse,* 132, 245; Fitts, "Mapping Catawba Coalescence," 10). After Traunter left the Suterees, he "steered from thence *South Easterly* about Two hundred Miles farther" (Traunter, *Travels,* Journal Two, 36).

† According to Kelton, the smallpox epidemic that swept the region between 1696 and 1700 was the region's first encounter with the disease, so its toll on the region's Indians was extremely deadly ("Great Southeastern Smallpox Epidemic," 21–22). Lawson reported no active smallpox outbreaks during his journey in 1701, but he noted that smallpox had recently killed numerous Sewees who lived at the mouth of the Santee River as well as Santees, whose village was north of Charleston, both locations lying south of the Suterees and Waxhaws where Traunter had encountered an active outbreak (*New Voyage,* 17). Comparing the accounts of Traunter and Lawson shows the wide arc of devastation but not whether the Sewees and Santees were ill at the same time as the more northerly Indians. Lawson noted that the Santees had "lost much of their former numbers" to smallpox (*New Voyage,* 34, 231–32).

‡ Lawson depicted the same immersion process and deadly effect (*New Voyage,* 17).

least Sixteen Miles long and almost as Broad, We continued here Two Days being Saturday & Sunday.

MUNDAY THE 18TH. [OF SEPTEMBER]

We Sett out from the Suterees and travell'd till we came to a Nation of Indians called the *Waterees*,* This Nation litle differing from the *Suterees* in Language, These people treated us very civilly, being just come in from hunting As we came there, feasting us with Venison Turkeys, and Bears flesh which is the best of food, We continued here Tuesday & Wednesday by reason that it rained very hard in so much that we could not travell.

THURSDAY THE 21TH. [OF SEPTEMBER]

We sett out from the Waterees, and travell'd till we came to a Nation of Indians called the Wax-aw's,† Though These Nations are Soe near to each other They Speak a quite different Language, The Small Pox haveing kill'd Severall in this Town and Such Sorrowfull lamenting for the deceased as I never Saw, For the Indian that has lost any Relation will goe to the Grave and Sitt upon it for the Space of four houres every Day for att least a Month after the Buriall. Att this Town I had the Oportunity of Seeing an Indian Buriall which was of a Child [29] about Six years old being the Warr-Captains' Son, The manner of which was as followeth. The Child was very ill when I came to the Town; The Indian Doctor useing his uttmost Endeavour to recover the Child by carrying him severall times into the Sweating house, and plungeing him into the cold Water that before night he dyed; There was Such howling and Crying that I could not Sleep that night. [P]

The next day continueing their Sorrow in a greater Measure than the day before, Att length about Three of the Clock in the Afternoon The Indian Doctor thought fitt that he Should be buried, and accordingly he diggs the Grave, and when he had digg'd it about four foot Deep much like unto an English

---

* Traunter's Wateree Town was located around present-day Lancaster, South Carolina, about 26 miles southeast of the Suteree town near Sugar Creek. Beck located Lawson's Waterees about 60 miles north of the Congarees, or in roughly the same area as Traunter's Waterees (Beck, *Chiefdoms, Collapse,* 165, 246; Swanton, *Indians of the Southeastern United States,* 205).

† This Waxhaw town was 28 miles southeast of the Waterees, suggesting a location southeast of the current town of Taxahaw in Lancaster County, South Carolina.

Grave in Shape, The length and breadth being proportionable to the person to be buried therein, After he had digged this plain grave he digged a place into one Side of the firm ground, not digging it perpendicular but Shelveing into the Side of the grave right from the Bottom,* into which Cavity they putt abundance of Indian corn and Pease, together with a Gourd full of Bear's Oyle to grease his hair withall, and a litle piese of Red-Lead and Vermilion to paint himself, Together with a litle Kettle to boyle his corn and Pease, and a Spoon and a knife. There was also put into the Cavity about a pound of Beads and a great many Bells like morrice Dancer's Bells, and upon his head a Garland of fine feathers, Haveing putt into the Cavity all the Materialls aforesaid; Then was brought the Child being layd upon a large Buck Skinn and Two Duffil'd Blanketts under that, and two Buck-Skins over him [30] being of the best leather they could gett, to the End that when he arose in the other world those Skins might be to make him shoes to hunt and travell in: Haveing layd him in his Grave they putt in to it his Bow and a Quiver full of Arrows, When they begann to throw in the Earth An Indian fired five Gunns over him, after that the Grave was filled up, Then I asked an Indian why they did not putt the Child into the Cave that they had digg'd in the Side of the Grave, And he told me their Design was that no Body might easily come and take his Victualls from him, when as he Stood Centry between; That being the chieff end of this Cupboard, [P]

I also ask'd the Indian Slave that I had with me the reason they used Such Ceremonies, and what Thoughts they had of the world to come, which they thought the Child was in all probability goeing to, And he told me the Opinion of the Indians was, that when they depart this world, that they doe not dye but Sleep for a time, The which Time being expired they Soon arrive at a brave Spacious Countrey where there is abundance of Deer, Bear, Turkeys and all Sort of Game in Such plenty, that they cannot goe amiss for them: And this is all the Heaven that those poor Indians expect, and that they shall never dye again but hunt and glutt themselves as they did in this world,† We continued att this Indian Town Friday Saturday and Sunday.

* Coe depicted similar shaft-and-chamber burials at Town Creek and at the Fredericks archaeological site (Occaneechi) at Hillsborough (*Town Creek*, 352–55).

† The Indian afterlife Indian Jack described to Traunter was very similar to what Lawson said was a "Country of Souls" where the dead "never meet with Hunger, Cold, or Fatigue [and] every thing to answer his Expectation and Desire" (*New Voyage*, 187). Beverley called the Indian afterlife "their *Elizium*," a place "stor'd with the highest perfection of all their Earthly Pleasures," adding that it was "an everlasting Spring" (*History and Present State*,

JOURNAL ONE—1698

MUNDAY THE 25TH. [OF SEPTEMBER]

We Sett out from the Waxawes, and travell'd till we came to the Great Swamp, where we lay this Night.*

TUESDAY THE 26TH: [OF SEPTEMBER]

We Sett out from the great Swamp and travell'd till We came to the *High Rocks*,† we went out a hunting and killed some Turkeys and lay there this night.

[31] WEDNESDAY, THE 27TH. [OF SEPTEMBER]

We Sett out from the high Rocks and travell'd till we came to a place called the Guttling Creek,‡ where we went a hunting and killed a Deer. Thursday it rain'd Soe hard that we did not travell that Day; But went out a hunting and killed another Deer that Day, We lay there that night.

FRIDAY THE 28TH. [OF SEPTEMBER]§

We Sett out from the Guttling Creek and Travell'd till we came to the Bridge Creek.¶

---

159). This is analogous to the "perpetual spring" Ned Bearskin related to Byrd II ("Secret History of the Line," in *Prose Works*, 119).

* Great Swamp was part of Traunter's extended detour into the present-day South Carolina counties of Lancaster and Chesterfield. He returned to Great Swamp in 1699 (*Travels*, Journal Two, 48).

† Hanging Rock is a Lancaster County landmark that was on the Waxhaw Road. A 1752 plat shows the Indian path crossed Hanging Rock Creek "just a few hundred yards north of the rock," then continued south through Kershaw County into present-day Camden (Inabinet and Inabinet, *History of Kershaw County*, 36; Floyd, *Lancaster County*, 107).

‡ There are several possibilities for what Traunter called Guttling Creek: the Wateree River, Flat Rock Creek, or Little Flat Rock Creek, all in the vicinity of Camden, South Carolina. This was near the remains of Cofitachequi, now the Mulberry archaeological site (Beck, *Chiefdoms, Collapse*, 44–45). From Guttling Creek, Traunter followed the same route into Charleston on both journeys.

§ Thursday is missing from Traunter's account, but the dates are still consecutive. This day-date error is repeated until the end of the journal.

¶ Bridge Creek is near Elgin, a suburb of present-day Columbia, South Carolina.

SATURDAY THE 29TH. [OF SEPTEMBER]

We Sett out from the Bridge Creek and travell'd till we came to the *Congree River*, where we were much troubled in getting over our Goods and horses,* att length haveing gain'd the other Side We lay there att Some Indian houses† Sunday, and Munday, where there grew very large Pignutt Trees‡ which were overladen with Fruit, it being a curious Thinnshell'd Nutt in Shape like the English Wallnutt, but not soe bigg I doe believe the Trees were att least four foot Diameter. We gather'd abundance of this Fruit, and carried it with us on our journey which lasted us into *Carolina* though we eat plentifully of them every day.

TUESDAY OCTOBER THE 2D.

We Sett out from the Congree River, and travell'd till we came to a place where there was a very large lake,§ there being abundance of Cranes upon this Lake, And near this Lake there is a great Swamp where we lay that Night.

---

　* A plausible ford was by Granby Dam south of the Saluda River and Broad River confluence, at modern Columbia, South Carolina. The Granby Dam was constructed in the twentieth century to "provide at least a 4-foot navigation depth in the Congaree up to the city of Columbia" because naturally low water levels limited watersports (Wachob, "Impact of Removing Granby Dam," 1). A more northern crossing would have required Traunter to cross both the Broad and Saluda Rivers, and he only mentioned one crossing (Adams and Trinkley, "Archaeological Reconnaissance and Survey," 5).

　† Traunter did not indicate whether these "Indian houses" were part of an inhabited community or an abandoned one. It is possible that this was a Congaree village, or the remains of one. Lefler situated Lawson's Congaree Town at present-day Fort Motte, about a day's ride south of modern Cayce, South Carolina, where archaeologists discovered evidence of a village (Stephenson, *Basic Inventory of Archeological Sites*, 111–15; Lefler, introduction to *New Voyage*, xii).

　‡ Pignut hickory trees.

　§ Traunter identified this as Pond Swamp in 1698 but in 1699 as Savana Hutts. His mileage puts this near an archaeological site at Savany Hunt Creek in today's Calhoun County, South Carolina. The identity of the Indians who lived here is unknown (Stephenson, *Basic Inventory of Archeological Sites*, 49). Lawson's map identified a "Savanna" and "Indian hutts" further south on the Santee River.

JOURNAL ONE—1698

WEDNESDAY THE 3D. [OF OCTOBER]

We Sett out from the Pond Swamp, and travell'd till we came to a place called the Millers Creek,* Great Raines comeing down [32] from the Mountaines, made the Creek soe high that we could hardly find a Convenient passage over, att length we found a very good ffoard and pass'd to the other Side where we lay that Night.

THURSDAY THE 4TH. [OF OCTOBER]

We Sett out from Miller's Creek and travell'd till we came to Sante River;† In this River are very large *Alligators* or Crocodiles. This River abounds with great plenty of very good Fish; Upon this River is the best Land that I discover'd in all my Travells being large Fields or Savanaes, att least four or five miles long, Upon the River as rich Land as ever Plough was putt into, and the only place in all Carolina for makeing a good settlemt.

When we arrived here the water was Soe high that we could not foard over, but were forced to stay here from Thursday untill Wednesday following, before the waters were abated We were employ'd in hunting, in the Interim killing Several Turkeys and Cranes, crossing over to the other side, we were employ'd all Day in getting over the Goods and horses, carrying our Goods over in a Canoe which we had for that purpose, haveing come Safe to the other Side of the River, we went out a hunting, Not goeing five hundred yards from our Camp but we kill'd a Stately Doe and Severall Turkeys We continued here this Night.

---

* Traunter's mileage to Millers Creek is consistent with the Mill Creek northeast of Orangeburg that appears on Tanner's 1825 map, or the modern Bates Mill Creek (Tanner, *Map of North and South Carolina*). Bates Mill Creek is in the vicinity of modern Fort Motte, where Lefler placed Lawson's Congaree Town (Lefler, introduction to *New Voyage*, xii). In 1699 Traunter called this Tireing Branch because one of his horses "tired" after he "travell'd Soe hard" (*Travels*, Journal Two, 53–54).

† The Congaree River became the Santee River between present-day Vance and Eutaw Springs, or the point at which the river tracked sharply to the north and east. Traunter was on the west side of Congaree/Santee River and had to recross it to finish his journey into Charles Town. He considered this the South Carolina border. Lefler situated the Santee Indians Lawson visited at Eutaw Springs, which may be the "Indian Hutts" on Lawson's map (Lefler, introduction to *New Voyage*, xii). It was also where John Hearn established his plantation (Ivers, *Torrent of Indians*, 85).

THURSDAY THE 11TH. [OF OCTOBER]

We Sett out from Sante River and travell'd till we came to a place call'd Beaver Creek where we lay that night.

FRIDAY THE 12TH. [OF OCTOBER]

We Sett out from Beaver Creek and travell'd to the Bear Swamp.

[33] SATURDAY THE 13TH. [OF OCTOBER]

Wee Sett out from *Bear Swamp* and travell'd to Turkey Creek,* we lay there Sunday.

MUNDAY THE 15TH. [OF OCTOBER]

We Sett out from Turkey Creek and travell'd till we came to Captn. James Moor's† in Carolina the most part of this Land from Sante River being Sandy ground with Pine Trees very few Oak and Hiccary.

The End of my First Journal.

---

* Turkey Creek is northwest of Charleston; see Tanner, *Map of North and South Carolina*.

† James Moore lived on Goose Creek, then north of Charleston.

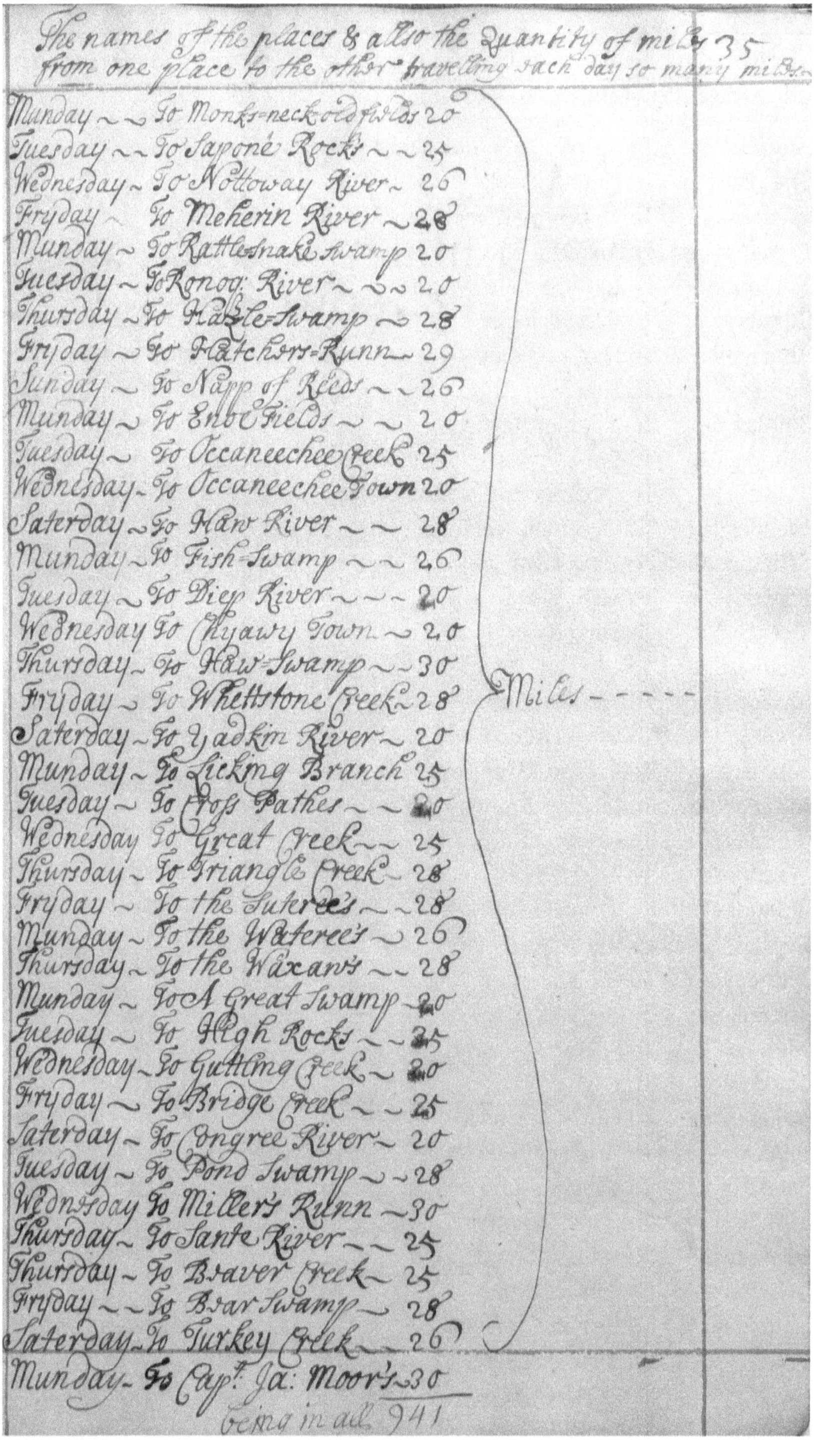

The names of the places & also the Quantity of miles 35
from one place to the other travelling each day so many miles

Munday	To Monks-neck old fields	20
Tuesday	To Saponé Rocks	25
Wednesday	To Nottoway River	26
Fryday	To Meherin River	28
Munday	To Rattlesnake Swamp	20
Tuesday	To Ronoo: River	20
Thursday	To Hazle-Swamp	28
Fryday	To Hatchers-Runn	29
Sunday	To Napp of Reeds	26
Munday	To Enoe Fields	20
Tuesday	To Occaneechee Creek	25
Wednesday	To Occaneechee Town	20
Saterday	To Haw River	28
Munday	To Fish Swamp	26
Tuesday	To Deep River	20
Wednesday	To Chyawy Town	20
Thursday	To Haw Swamp	30
Fryday	To Whettstone Creek	28
Saterday	To Yadkin River	20
Munday	To Licking Branch	25
Tuesday	To Cross Pathes	20
Wednesday	To Great Creek	25
Thursday	To Triangle Creek	28
Fryday	To the Suherees	28
Munday	To the Wateree's	26
Thursday	To the Waxaws	28
Munday	To A Great Swamp	20
Tuesday	To High Rocks	25
Wednesday	To Gutting Creek	20
Fryday	To Bridge Creek	25
Saterday	To Congree River	20
Tuesday	To Pond Swamp	28
Wednesday	To Millers Runn	30
Thursday	To Sante River	25
Thursday	To Beaver Creek	25
Fryday	To Bear Swamp	28
Saterday	To Turkey Creek	26
Munday	To Capt: Ja: Moor's	30

being in all 941

Miles - - - - -

Figure 2. Mileage chart for 1698, Traunter manuscript. (Virginia Museum of History and Culture, Mss5:9 T6945:1)

[35]

The names of the places & also the Quantity of miles from one place to the other travelling each day so many miles

Munday	To Monks-neck-old-fields	20
Tuesday	To Sapone Rocks	25
Wednesday	To Nottoway River	26
Fryday	To Meherin River	28
Munday	To Rattle-Snake Swamp	20
Tuesday	To Ronoq: River	20
Thursday	To Hazle-Swamp	28
Fryday	To Hatchers-Runn	29
Sunday	To Napp of Reeds	26
Munday	To Enoe Fields	20
Tuesday	To Occaneechee Creek	25
Wednesday	To Occaneechee Town	20
Saterday	To Haw River	28
Munday	To Fish-Swamp	26
Tuesday	To Diep River	20
Wednesday	To Chyawy Town	20
Thursday	To Haw-Swamp	30
Fryday	To Whettstone Creek	28
Saterday	To Yadkin River	20
Munday	To Licking Branch	25
Tuesday	To Cross Pathes	20
Wednesday	To Great Creek	25
Thursday	To Triangle Creek	28
Fryday	To the Suterees	28
Munday	To the Wateree's	26
Thursday	To the Waxaw's	28
Munday	To A Great Swamp	20
Tuesday	To High Rocks	25
Wednesday	To Guttling Creek	20
Fryday	To Bridge Creek	25
Saterday	To Congree River	20
Tuesday	To Pond Swamp	28
Wednesday	To Miller's Runn	30
Thursday	To Sante River	25
Thursday	To Beaver Creek	25
Fryday	To Bear Swamp	28
Saterday	To Turkey Creek	26
Munday	To Capt. Ja: Moor's	30
	being in all,	941

⟩ Miles ——

JOURNAL TWO—1699
An Exact Journal of my Second Journey from Virginia to South Carolina by Land Anno 1699

[From the Appomattox store almost to Occaneechi Town, Traunter's route was identical to that taken in 1698. Twenty miles from Occaneechi Town, he detoured to Ajusher in the vicinity of modern Durham, North Carolina. Eno Will led Traunter from Ajusher through what is today eastern North Carolina on a southerly route that ran between the Uwharrie Mountains and the Atlantic coast to what is now Fayetteville, North Carolina. At that point Traunter and Will headed west to the Yadkin River, then south again through present-day eastern South Carolina until their "new" road intersected with the Waxhaw Road north of today's Camden. The same route from Camden to Charleston was used for both journeys.]

[1] I embark'd att Charles Town in South Carolina the third of March 1699, and sailed into *Ronoque* Harbor[*] The 24th of the same Moneth, Being bound for Virg:a but being prevented by contrary winds I bought me A horse in *Ronoque*[†] and travell'd to Virginia by Land, arriveing there the 2d of Aprill, It being about One hundred and Eighty Miles from *Ronoque* to *Virginia;* and being very well pleased with the long journey I had before accomplish'd to *Carolina*, I was resolved once more to putt my Self in a capacity to undertake the Fatigue of the Second, In Order to which being well furnished with men, Horses, Arms, Amunition and Provision, I was resolved to find out (if possible) A nearer passage to Carolina then I had travell'd the first time, By reason in my first journey, I directed my course somewt near the *Appallatian* mountaines, my design thereby being to head the Rivers which I thought might not be so passable nearer the Sea, But being now more expert in Travel-

---

[*] Albemarle Sound in present-day North Carolina.
[†] Bath, North Carolina. Two Collet maps show a path/road going north into Virginia from Bath: *Map of North Carolina* and *Map of the Southern Part of North Carolina.*

ling and desirous of farther discoveries, I imagin'd that those Rivers might be passable in Some places nigher the [2] Sea and therefore was resolved to discover that passage which I was well satisfied must cutt short my first journey by a very great many Miles, There being another Conveniency in this Journey, by reason that wee avoyded A great deale of trouble in not travelling through the Indians Corn as we did the first Journey, Our horses destroying much of it to their great losse, Our Road lying just through their Corn fields that we could not help it. Those and severall other Considerations engaged me to make A New Discovery, To which I shall proceed in order as followeth. But it is to be noted that in my first journey to *Carolina*, I travell'd along the *Virginia* Traders path from one Indian Town to another, which consequently must be farther about than if I had gone a direct Course, also Steering West for att least Six hundred miles to a Nation of Indians called the *Suterees* And then altering my Course I steered from thence *South Easterly* about Two hundred Miles farther, Then altering my Course as the path lead me steering *A South* and by *West* Course againe for tw days journey, Then the path steer'd South and by East into *Carolina*, And steering Such wild Courses in my first journey I was persuaded that if I steered more direct and could but passe the Rivers it would be much nearer, which I performed and accordingly it proved Soe.

Setting out from Appomattox River in *Virginia* on Munday ye 1st of Septembr Anno 1699: We came to Monck's-Neck where we lay that night.*

[3] TUESDAY YE 2D. OF SEPTEMBER 1699†

We sett out from Monks'-Neck and travell'd till we came to the Sapone Spring, where we went out a hunting and killed Some Turkeys lying there that Night.

WEDNESDAY YE 3D. OF SEPTR.

We Sett out from the *Sapone* spring and travell'd till we came to *Notoway* River, where we lay that night.

---

* In 1699 the men (and thirty-six horses) who left Appomattox River with Traunter and his servant were likely Solomon Legaré and Henry Netherton, as well as an unidentifiable man.

† Traunter's days and dates mostly align with the New Style (Gregorian) calendar in this 1699 journal, but he was consistently off by one day (Cheney, *Handbook*, 11, 140–41, table 29). Traunter's entries are briefer for this segment of travel than in 1698, perhaps to avoid repetitiveness.

JOURNAL TWO—1699

THURSDAY YE 4 [OF SEPTEMBER]

We Sett out from Notoway River, and travell'd till we came to Meherin* river, We went a hunting and kill'd severall Turkeys, We lay here this night. But we could not Sleep for the Howling of Wolves which walk'd around us all night very near to our Camp, But came not within Gunn-shott.

FRIDAY YE 5TH. [OF SEPTEMBER]

We sett out from *Meherin* River and travell'd till we came to *Ronoque River*, The ffoard† being very low so that we ffoarded over without much difficulty, We kill'd Some wild Ducks being the Ducke and Mallard sort, and about halfe a Dozen Teales very fatt, We continued here Saturday and Sunday.

MUNDAY YE 8TH. [OF SEPTEMBER]

We Sett out from *Ronoque* River and travell'd till we came to *Hatchers-runn*.

TUESDAY YE 9TH. [OF SEPTEMBER]

We Sett out from *Hatcher's-Run* and travell'd till We came to the *Nap-of-Reeds*,‡ where we went a hunting and kill'd A Turkey We lay here this Night.

WEDNESDAY YE 10TH. [OF SEPTEMBER]

We Sett out from the Nap-of-Reeds and travell'd till we came to Geniton-Tar-river,§ where we went a hunting and kill'd Some Turkeys lying here this Night.

---

* No stop was recorded between the Meherrin and Roanoke Rivers. In 1698 he stopped at Rattlesnake Swamp. The mileage between the rivers was the same for both trips, and he was on the same path.

† Moniseep Ford on the Roanoke River near present Henderson, North Carolina (Davis, "Cultural Landscape," 152).

‡ Hatcher's Run is north of modern Durham, North Carolina. Knap of Reeds Creek is near today's Stem, North Carolina. Traunter was still using the same route he took in 1698.

§ The Geniton-Tar River was listed in Traunter's 1698 journal as well, but there is no record of a Geniton-Tar River. In 1698 Traunter described this as Eno Fields, a village destroyed by Tuscaroras (*Travels*, Journal One, 18).

[4] THURSDAY YE 11TH. [OF SEPTEMBER]

We sett out from *Geniton-Tar River* and travell'd till we came to *Doe Swamp*,* haveing travell'd in the Same path hitherto as we did in our first journey, And understanding by the *Virginia* Traders whom I mett here,† yt my old Friend *King Enoe Will* being the Indian that in my first journey I gave the Commission or as he called it the *Soc-ca-hick* to; was then removed from the *Occaneechee* Town, The Virg:a Traders were very glad to See me, and withall told me, That the Occaneechees had driven their King Enoe Will from Amongst them not Suffering him to gather his corn that he had planted before he departed from them, And the Chieff Cause that the Occaneechees had rebelled against Enoe-Will was, as they sayd, because he had lost his Commission For whilst he had his *Soc-ca-hick* they all dreaded him and were very obedient to his Commands, meerly through the fear that they bore to his Commission, imagining that there was Something more than ordinary in the paper, alsoe ye Occaneechees could never endure Enoe Will because that he loved the English, That as Soon as ever they knew that he had lost his Commission They forthwith expell'd him, And when he departed from the Occaneechees Some of them that had any Affection for him march'd off with him, And Severall Indians of other Adjacent Nations that heard of his being expell'd by the Occaneechees, mett him at a place called Ajusher,‡ where with A mutuall Consent they joyned themselves under [5] His government and built A Town in that place, Enoe Will desiring the *Virginia* Traders to tell

---

* This is the place Traunter called Occaneechee Creek in 1698. He left the Occaneechi Path/main trade road here.

† Doe Swamp/Occaneechee Creek was 25 miles (one day) from Occaneechi Town but only 10 miles from Ajusher. Lawson said Ajusher was 14 miles from Occaneechi Town (*New Voyage*, 62). Ajusher seemed to be in the vicinity of present-day Durham, North Carolina. Traunter's spelling of Ajusher varied: Ajusher, Adjusheere (in the 1699 mileage log), and Ajusheres when he referred to the people (*Travels*, Journal One, 23).

‡ After an archaeological investigation in 1973, in the floodplain of the Falls Reservoir project on the Neuse River, and by comparing archaeological artifacts and Lawson's account, Keel and Coe situated Ajusher on the Flat River near where it is crossed by state highway 1004 and concluded that Ajusher was in the flood zone northeast of modern Durham, North Carolina ("Reconnaissance and Proposal," 11). Using Lawson's description that Ajusher was due east of the Occaneechi Town at present Hillsborough, Rights thought Ajusher was on a creek "northwest of the present city of Durham" (*American Indian*, 87). Briceland placed Ajusher at a Shakori village on New Hope Creek south of Durham, outside the flood zone, which is consistent with Traunter's mileage (phone conversation with the editor).

me his misfortunes and that he wanted A Commission very much, because the Occaneechees were grown as bad as ever to the English, The Traders also entreated me that I would goe to Ajusher and give Enoe Will another Commission, or else they believed there would be noe tradeing with the Indians in those parts (especially the Occaneechees,) haveing promised the Traders that I would goe to Ajusher to give Enoe Will A Commission, And alsoe that I would further their Trade as much as in my power lay, I parted with them and travell'd to the *Doe Swamp* and lay there that night.

FRIDAY YE 12TH. [OF SEPTEMBER]

We Sett out from the Doe-Swamp and travell'd till we came to Ajusher, the Indians being transported with joy that I was come and found ym out in that obscure place, when haveing invited me into their houses and treated me with the best they had I ask'd them where Enoe Will their king was, They told me he was out a hunting I ordered ym to Send one of their best runners for him And to tell him that I had another Soc-ca-hick for him, which is to be remembered was the Name they gave the Commission, that noe Sooner had the Indians heard the word but they hasted the Runner [6] with such dispatch That one would have thought he hardly travell'd the Ground he made Such Expedition. The Runner haveing deliver'd his Errand to Enoe Will, telling him that I was in his Town, and stayed for him, Enoe Will being over joy'd att this News took up some of his Venison that he had kill'd, returning with the Runner and ordering his men to make all possible speed after him, for he rann all the way and Soon arrived att his Town, where he painted and dressed himself after the best manner according to their Custome, and in his best Robes, which was A Coat of party-coloured Red and blew Cloth, with Copper Lace,* and Glasse Buttons, and a great many Beads about his neck, with A great Shell on his breast. And in this Dresse with his face painted Red wth Vermillion, and round his Eyes wore Circles of blacke, And A black Stroake down his Forehead, nose and Chinn, And his Hair all greaz'd wth Bear's Oyle, and two Eagles Feathers very long sticking upright in his Ears, haveing great holes in them for that purpose, And he came to our Camp haveing order'd his man to bring half A Deer to present me withal, Att the Kings arrival he express'd very great joy to See me. And haveing shew'd much friendship to each

---

* Copper denoted status in Native societies. According to Oberg, "only *weroances* and their closest advisors wore it" (*Head in Edward Nugent's Hand,* 46).

other after very [7] many Indian complements pass'd between us, I ask'd him how he had govern'd the Nations Since I parted with him, in my first journey to *Carolina,* And whether he had gott his Soc-ca-hick or commission with him yett, that I had given him in my other Journey, To which he reply'd with A sorrowfull Countenance, that he had A great misfortune. [P]

One day being in eager Chace of A Bear that he had shott att running hastily through the Bushes he lost his Poutch wherein was his Soc-ca-hick, when returning home to the Occaneeches Town, The Occaneechees by some means came to know that he had lost his Soc-ca-hick, and began to grow rebellious Rogues and would not own him for their King, And to be brieff ask'd him what Businesse he had there, commanding him to be gone Since he had lost his Soc-ca-hick or they sayd they'd kill him, so that the King was forced to rubb off from among them to the place where he now lives, I farther ask'd him if I should give him Another Commission, whether he'd venture to goe and rule the Occaneechees again or continue there with those few he had gott, To which he answer'd me That he would not be afrayd to goe to the Occaneechees, But he sayd He'd never be king of such Rogues again. Also he told me [8] He hoped that in A short time he should be powerfull enough to goe and make Warr upon them, vowing to kill every man, woman and Child of them, calling them all the ill names he could thinke on, ffor sayd he the Occaneechees Sayd that if ever they could by any possible means putt me out of the Way, The next thing they'd doe should be to kill all the English they could. And here he told me the whole Account of Robert Stephens' death, as followeth. [P]

Robert Stevens and his Company, as is before related, haveing as they thought secured themselves on a Small Necke of Land, and knowing noe Indians to be nigher them than A Nation called the *Meherrins,* which was about a hundred Miles distant from them,* But there happen'd att that time to be, a party of *Tomahittans*† to be a hunting near to a Nation of Indians called the Occaneechees, which Nation the *Virginians* trade withal, These Carolina men haveing come by this Nation of the Occaneechees, and lay'n in their

---

* The Meherrins were Iroquoian-speaking Indians who lived near the Virginia–North Carolina border, east of the Occaneechis. By the 1670s they were recognized as one of Virginia's tributary tribes (Briceland, *Westward from Virginia,* 2).

† Tomahittans were referenced in Abraham Wood's retelling of Needham and Arthur's journey. Davis identified the Tomahittans as Cherokees ("Travels of Needham and Arthur," 31). Waselkov argues that the Tomahittans were Hitchiti-speaking people from Georgia ("Seventeenth-Century Trade," 118).

Town one night, which gave them oportunity to View their Arms and Clothes and would willingly have murder'd the men that night for what they had, but another thought possessing them that if they should kill those men, (reasoning thus with themselves) that the Traders comeing among them would See the men's Clothes, and Armes, and therefore would make Warr upon them and kill them, att length perceiveing that they could by noe undiscovered [9] means performe this wicked Art themselves, They thought of those *Tamohittans* that were then not many miles off from their Towne a hunting, haveing Deer-Skins and ffurrs good-Store, Upon this Consideration they called A Councill of Warr, as they call it, for in matters of moment there is nothing to be done without it, and their Grandee man or Warr Captaine as they call him Standing up he thus proposed unto them the Matter.

That it is sayd he, possible enough for us to be partakers of this Booty, thô not actually the murderers; nor yett to keep any of the Clothes or Arms belonging to those Englishmen, but that we will make an Agreement with the Tomahittans, that they Shall goe and kill those men, And bring unto their hunting Stage the whole Booty, where we will be in readynesse against their returne to divide the Spoyle, The Tomahittans giveing us Deer-Skins and ffurrs for our Shares and they keeping the things belonging to the English for their Share, by reason they doe not trade with the English, And therefore may doe this without the least Suspition on their Side likewise.

Then spoke another of the Grandees, and Sayd it was a very good proposall, provided the Tamohittans would but Effect it, Another replied Theres no question but yt they will, For the Tamohittans dwelling near to New-Yorke* use money in trading with the English there, and that for what money these [10] Men have they will not be Suspected for by the English, And indeed 'tis too true that there is not any *Nation* of *Indians* in America that make any Scruple of killing the English when they can safely doe it, But to be brieff, Noe sooner had the Grandee made this Reply, But they were all striveing who should goe and informe the Tamohittans For says one I can runn best, and another he could runn best, The Devil prompting them they could all runn best, Notwithstanding one was Sent, And noe Sooner delivered his Errand but it was as readily accepted with abundance of Satisfaction on both sides, So that they that the Tamohittans had appointed for the Murderers returned with the Messenger to the Occaneechees Town and were received with great

---

* Traunter implied Five Nations Iroquoian affiliation when he said the Tomahittans were from New York.

joy, and the promises being again related to them, and very well approved off, they made a Warr Dance as it is generally their Custome, before they undertake any Action, and Soe dismissed them and they appointed to be the murderers Dogg'd the Carolina men, untill they came to that place aforementioned where the men had appointed for to lodge that Night, [P]

The Murderers Seeing them from an obscure place where they lay in Ambush, And the manner that those men order'd their Affaires before they lay down to Sleep, The Murderers haveing Clubbs on purpose for their designe, Sent one of their company out about Midnight to See, and discover, whether the men were Sound asleep or noe, when returning again to his Companions, told [11] them that was the time to doe their businesse in, then they all imediately gott upon their hands and knees carrying their Clubbs in their Teeth, which were not above two foot and a halfe in length, there being but five men of them, one of which had a Gunn the other four Clubbs, when they came very near unto the place where the Carolina men lay, the Indian that had the Gunn, discharg'd it as near as he could aime att Robert Stephens As we Suppose. The Gunn being loaded with Ball, Shott ye Indian Slave through the Thigh, passing by John Herne, went through Robert Stevens' head, & imediately fell in with their Clubbs that they imediately dispatch'd him, Enoe Will haveing told me this, I order'd him to call A Councill of Warr to the End that I might give him A Soc-ca-hick or Commission haveing it ready writ, He desired me to sitt downe with my men on one side of the fire, and his men Sitting down on the other side of the fire, which was made in the midst of his house, He then placed himself just by me, Then he haveing commanded Silence, I tooke the Commission in my hand, and told them in the Tusk-aurora Language, that by virtue of this Soc-ca-hick, they must as Soon as they thought fitt, goe to the *Tusk-Aurora Indians,* and to tell them that I had given *Enoe Will* the Soc-ca-hick to the end that they might come and assist him in killing the Occaneechees, if they should hurt the English or disturb them in their Trade, Since they had been Such Rogues as to say they would kill the English. Haveing thus putt them in A Method [12] how to kill their and our Enemies, I delivered the Soc-ca-hick to Enoe Will, and told him that my designe was to find out a nearer passage to *Carolina* than that Journey I first travell'd was, to which he Answer'd That if I would accept of him and his mans Company to hunt for me, He was ready to venture his life with me upon the Discovery, which I readily embraced, *Enoe Will* and his man was furnish'd with all things necessary to undergoe the Fatigue of A discovery. Haveing stayed here Saturday and Sunday to regulate this State Affair.

JOURNAL TWO—1699

MUNDAY YE 15TH. [OF SEPTEMBER]

We Sett out from Ajusher haveing taken our leave of this Small Government travelling till we came to the Haw-River,* haveing Six Indian Hunters besides the King and his man to convoy us to this River, where we parted with the Six Men, The King and his man being fully resolv'd to endure the Fatigue of this journey—On each Side of this River the Land is Hilly and Stoney, wth Oaks Hiccary and Pine Trees.

TUESDAY YE 16TH. [OF SEPTEMBER]

We Sett out from the Haw-River and travell'd till we came to the resolute Swamp,† where we all went out a hunting but kill'd nothing, here We consulted what course to Steere the next day, and concluded to Steere a South and by West Course.

WEDNESDAY YE 17TH. [OF SEPTEMBER]

We Sett out from Resolute-Swamp, and travell'd till we came to the Diep River,‡ In this days journey the King rideing before us, Spied a Rattlesnake, and called out to us to turne our [13] horses another way, which when wee had done he shott him, after the King had kill'd the Snake I alight from my horse and open'd the Snake with my knife, He haveing a whole Squirrell in his Belly not a hair of him being diminished, it being common for them to Swallow a hare which is much larger than a Squirrell, haveing come to the above sayd River We went out a hunting and kill'd severall Turkeys, alsoe killing Some Teal, which were on this River in great Quantities, The Indian King and his Man being very Serviceable to us For as Soon as We came to the River, We pitched our Camp on the first convenient place; The King employ'd himself in walking

---

* Traunter may have crossed the Haw River north of Upper Cane Creek, farther downriver than where the main trade road crossed it. Collet's later map shows a path near there (*Map of North Carolina*).

† Based on Traunter's directional information, Resolute Swamp was probably around modern Snow Camp, North Carolina.

‡ Traunter crossed the Deep River downstream from his 1698 crossing and, based on Collet's map (1770), may have done so around modern Franklin or Ramseur. Traunter's route south ran east of the Uwharrie Mountains. Collet indicated two possible paths that roughly paralleled the course of the Little River, which intersected with an east-west path at Cross Creek, today's Fayetteville, North Carolina (Crittenden, "Overland Travel," 243).

up the River Side to find out a good foarding place for us to goe over The next Morning, when returning he brought with him A Turkey, telling us he had found out a very good foard for us to goe over the River, in this days' journey A Kennell of Wolves mett us, running up directly towards us, The Bushes being so thicke that they did not see us before they came within Twenty yards of us, There being att least fourteene of them, that fireing among them as I sate upon my horse kill'd one of them, which was very large the rest running away.

THURSDAY YE 18TH. [OF SEPTEMBER]

We Sett out from Diep River, foarding altogether as well over there as we did higher up in our first journey, We travell'd from hence to a place called the Foaling Runn,* The next morning being Friday one of my Mares Foaled a stately Mare Foal. I and my men disputed much what we should doe with the Foal, for Some would [14] have it kill'd, and some would have it Saved, But if we had Saved it We could not stay till it might be able to travaile, For We could not tell how long our journey might be, and being upon A new Discovery We could not tell how our provision might last, So that We thought it most convenient to kill the Foal and eat him, Which accordingly We did, (Eating very well,) For We had Bacon that wee brought with us, and boyling a piece of that with Some of the Foale made incomparable good Broth, We continued here this day, being for the most part employ'd in Barbicuing our Foal, which was after this manner. We cut four forkes which were abt four foot long and Sharpening the Ends We drove them into the ground, and then laying Small Sticks a-crosse them cutting our meat into thinn Slices, We put it upon this Hurdle, haveing A great Wood fire That was quite burnt downe to Coales, not one Smoaking stick being left under the Hurdle, Soe that our meat roasted very well, which being done we carried What we could not eat along with us, we lay here this Night.

SATURDAY YE 20TH. [OF SEPTEMBER]

We Sett out from the Foaling-Run, and travell'd till We came to the *Raven-Run*,† where we had not been an hour, But the Ravens came croaking over us

---

* Coincidentally, a Barbecue Creek appears on eighteenth-century maps of this area and is still known as such.

† Raven Run was likely located around Cross Creek (now Fayetteville, North Carolina) where the southerly road may have terminated after it intersected with the east-west route that went toward the Yadkin River and Town Creek (Crittenden, "Overland Travel," 243).

as if they would have carried us away, In this days journey our Indian King kill'd a Deer, One of my men being A French Man, haveing a great Mind to the Blood that lay in the Belly of the Deer when [15] he was open'd, designing if he could have gott any thing to have carried the Blood in, to make a pudding out att night, but could not invent any manner of Conveniency to carry the Blood But was goeing to carry it in his hatt, which when I understood I told him he had better take the Maw of the Deer and empty out the Excrement and put the Blood in that, & that would alsoe Serve us for a pudding bagg to boyle it in, Yes sayes he this is a right Soldier Shift, and your Advice is very Seasonable, Soe he putt the Blood into the Maw and tieing it with a good Strong String, carried it att his Belt & being come to the Raven-Run above mentioned where we lay that night, The King and his man with all Speed made a good Fire, and fill'd our Kettle with Water putting it upon the Fire, and We putt into the Kettle our Indian pudding and Some venison, and when boyl'd they fell too, and eat up pudding, Bagg, and all, and left me ne're a Bitt of it, I being a hunting, They sayd Twas as good a pudding as ever they eat, We continued here Sunday—This days journey was for the most part hilly with Oak Hiccary and Pine Trees with abundance of Vines.

MONDAY THE 22TH. [OF SEPTEMBER]

We Sett out from the Raven Run, and travell'd till we came to a place call'd the Milky Run, where our Mare that had [16] lost the Foal Supplied us with good Store of Milke, We did not trouble our selves to goe out a hunting here, We had Venison enough left. The Ground continued Still hilly and but indifferent Land.

TUESDAY YE 23TH. [OF SEPTEMBER]

We Sett out from the Milky-Run, and travell'd till we came to the Yadkin alias Cape Fear River, where We found a very good Foard much better than the upper Foard wch we went over in our first journey to *Carolina*, It not being above our horses knees.* And haveing pitch'd our Camp on the other-side,

---

* Collet's map had the east-west route from Cross Creek cross the Yadkin River, near the present-day town of Mount Gilead, itself located near the Town Creek site that was still intermittently occupied in the late seventeenth century (Coe, *Town Creek*, 15, 18, 336; Boudreaux, *Archaeology of Town Creek*, 54–55, 111–12).

We went out a hunting and kill'd Severall Turkeys, and wild Ducks, up on the side of the River As I was a hunting I saw abundance of Rich Land, Not any Indians inhabiting thereabouts, But between us and the Sea A Nation of Indians called the *Wacawn's*,[*] being Caniballs, and Maneaters, But we Saw not any of them.

WEDNESDAY YE 24TH. [OF SEPTEMBER]

We Sett out from the Yadkin River travelling till we came to A River, which emptied itself into the Yadkin River, comeing down the Neck of Land which was made by the two Rivers, We happen'd to drive Three Bears before us, which when we had driven them that they could goe noe further for the Rivers that mett them, They [17] swam over this River that emptied itself into the Yadkin, for in our first journey to *Carolina,* We discover'd noe Such River, Soe that my men were for calling it the New River, But I told them we would rather call it the *Ursa-River,* because when the Bears were a swimming over it they all discharged their guns att them but kill'd none, about half a Mile up this River We found a very good Foarding place, being come to the other side we mett with a very great Swamp which proved very troublesome to us and our horses, For the grape vines were soe thick, that our horses could hardly goe twenty yards But they would be hang'd fast in the vines, soe that we were forced to cutt them loose with our hangers, putting forward from this River, we travell'd till we came to the Fishing Creek,[†] where there were inumerable Sholes of Fish very large as also abundance of Teale, Our Indian King and his man goeing out a hunting kill'd some Turkeys, We also killed store of fish, and Teal, fareing very sumptuously here.

THURSDAY YE 25TH. [OF SEPTEMBER]

We Sett out from the *Fishing Creek* and travell'd till we came to a great Swamp att least two miles through, The vines which were loaded with Clusters of Red/Black Grapes, There being noe white grapes in all the Woods in the Countrey, and underwood being so thicke that we could scarce rush through

---

[*] Woccon Indians. According to Lawson, two Woccon villages, Yupwauremau and Tooptatmeer, were on the lower Neuse River, east of Traunter's location (*New Voyage,* 242). See also Swanton, *Indians of the Southeastern United States,* 207–8.

[†] Fishing Creek may have been near present-day Wadesboro, North Carolina; Traunter's route seemed to parallel today's I-74.

them, att length gaining [18] The other side We encamp'd on the side of a Creeke, where we went a hunting and kill'd Some Turkeys, Two of my Men falling out wee called it the Quarrelling Creek, where wee lay that Night.*

FRIDAY THE 26TH. [OF SEPTEMBER]

We Sett out from Quarrelling Creek and travell'd till We came to a very Sandy Sort of Lande,† and could not find any Water to take up our Lodgings att, till our Indian King att length discover'd a small Puddle of Water in a Great Reedy Branch, Soe that we pitch'd there this Night, and were reasoning with our selves where wee might be, for by the Quality of the Land, One while We imagined that we were very near the Sea, And other times thinking we were very near the Waxaw Indians' Trading Path,‡ which we went in the first Journey to *Carolina*, calling it the Doubtfull Branch,§ Here I took the Barke off some Great Pine Trees, there growing no other Sort of Wood on this Land, and on the places that were made white, I putt up my name with Lamb-black¶ as alsoe the day of the moneth and date of the year, Every one of the men likewise Barked Trees and writt their names with the date &c, Then the Indian King he would have another fancy, There being a Tree that grew So as the Topp of it leaned downe within Twenty [19] foot off the Ground, We were a considerable while contriving a way how to gett hold of the Top of the Tree, to bend it down as we might tie Somewhat or other to the Top of it, and then lett it goe up again to the End that it might be for A monument to direct any others that might travell that way, Att length with abundance of trouble

---

* Traunter's mileages suggest Quarrelling Creek was in the area of present-day Wingate and Marshville, North Carolina.

† Marine sand surface soil is a unique topographical feature of the land between Big Black Creek and Little Lynches River in South Carolina's Chesterfield and Lancaster Counties, a region rich in silver and gold deposits (Pardee and Park, "Map of the Central Piedmont Region," in Roberts, *Carolina Gold Rush*; Foley and Ayuso, "Gold Deposits of the Carolina Slate Belt"; Dahlberg, "To the Common Good," 332–33).

‡ The Waxhaw Road, which Traunter took in 1698, roughly paralleled the Wateree River from modern Lancaster, South Carolina, south into Camden.

§ Doubtful Branch was probably near today's towns of Taxahaw and Jefferson in South Carolina.

¶ Lamp-black was a durable form of carbon used to identify property boundaries and for directional signage. "No other European colonists considered establishing private property or boundaries in the New World as central to legitimate possession" from lamp-black boundary markers to fencing (Seed, *Ceremonies of Possession*, 24).

We gott the Topp of it downe, by passing a long Rope-over, Then we asked our Indian King what we must doe next, Then he order'd one of my men to cutt down a Pine tree that was about five Inches Diameter, and about Twenty foot long, which he then did, and afterwards Squared it, and upon one of the Edges He ordered him to cutt a Notch for every man of us, and upon another Edge to cutt a Notch for every horse, There being in all Seaven men, and Six and Thirty horses and Mares, haveing Soe done wee tooke a New Rope and Slung this Twenty foot peice just by the middle like a ballance, and tied it fast to the Top of the Tree that we had bent down, and then lett goe the Tree Soe that it sprung up to its old place again, The peice with the Notches being poysed in the Ayr, made a figure that mightily [20] pleased the Indians, and if ever English or Indians should come that way, They would wonder how we could gett that peice up soe high.

SATURDAY THE 27TH. [OF SEPTEMBER]

We sett out from the doubtfull Branch, and travell'd to a path, we went in it about five miles imagining it to be the old trading path that we went in our first journey, for it being such Land as yt was; att length travelling soe farr, and finding noe place we had lodged att in our first Journey, we were then convinced of our Error and therefore tooke Our Lodgeing upon the side of A great Swamp,* disputing still what path this should be, So that I asked one of the men that had been with me in my first journey, whether he'd venture along with me if we went along that path, till such time as we should come to some Indian settlement, To which consequently this path must tend, where we might be informed whether we were right or noe, To which he readily replyed that he would venture his life with me, And where I dyed he'd dye too, being thus resolved I order'd two of the best horses [21] I had to be made ready, and We tooke Tenn Biskett each with us, and being armed with our Guns, Pistolls, and Swords, We took leave of our Company (telling them) that they must not expect us backe again till we had found some Indians, vowing to travell as long as We had one Biskett left, or one Grain of Amunition to kill meat, haveing took our leave we mounted and travell'd about sixteen miles upon a white sand, then the Land began to alter and we came to the Top of a high Rocky hill, The path continueing plaine and discoverable enough att

---

* In 1698 Traunter camped at "A Great Swamp," that mileages (and his language above) suggest is this location, but he listed it as Path Swamp in the 1699 mileage log.

JOURNAL TWO—1699

going down the Hill the path grew wider and plainer, that we had not travell'd five hundred paces before we discovered Indian Corne, keeping our path still, for we knew there could not be corne but there must be Indians, The path imediately ledd us up to the houses, [P]

The men being all out a hunting, but two whom we found att a play or Game they have among them called Chance, which is with little sticks in nature of Cards,* The women that were there ran as soon as ever they saw us to the Eno men that were at play, they being surpriz'd for there never were any English [22] men att that place before, The two men came running as fast as they could, being very neat limb'd men both, I ask'd them in the Wateree Language what people they were, and it happened they understood the Wateree Language, They told me that they were a remnant of *Waxawes*,† I then discours'd them in their own Language, They being mighty kind to us giveing us green Corne roasted in the Ear, which was very acceptable to us, and We gave them some of our Biskett which they took as a great favour, Then I told them that the rest of my Company was within Twenty Miles of their Towne, and that they were bound to stay there till I return'd to them again, Then I ask'd them how farr it was to the trading path, and they told me within one days journey from thence,‡ I then asked them whether they would goe with me back to my Company, telling them that King Enoe Will and his man were with us, it seems that these Indians heard the fame of Enoe Will with his Socca-hick or Comission and departing from thence the two Indians run before our horses all the Way till wee came to our Camp, My people being over joy'd to see us return'd so soon, King Enoe Will and [23] his man greeting those two Indians that came with us from the litle Town, and my men haveing kill'd a Deer and Two Turkeys for our Entertainment, the Two Waxaw-Indians stay'd with us that Night in order to goe with us to their own Town the next day.

---

* This game is similar to a gambling game Lawson described as a fast-paced "sort of Arithmetick" using fifty-one "small split Reeds." He claimed, "A good Sett of these Reeds" were worth "a dress'd Doe-Skin" (*New Voyage*, 178–80). Lawson mentioned gaming, generally, at the Congaree Town and "Chenco," or Chunky at Ajusher (34, 62).

† Traunter's statement that the people in this "litle" village were a "remnant of Waxawes," needs to be understood in relation to Wright's identification of Waxhaws as one of the "Cofitachequi remnants," peoples who had once been part of the powerful Cofitachequi paramount chiefdom, as were the Esaws, Waterees, Sugarees, Catawbas, Congarees and Santees (J. L. Wright, *Only Land*, 119). Cofitachequi, now the Mulberry archaeological site, was just south of today's Camden (Beck, *Chiefdoms, Collapse*, 44).

‡ "Within one days journey" means the main Waxhaw Road (from Hanging Rock to Camden) was less than 20 miles south of the little Waxhaw village.

SUNDAY 28TH. [OF SEPTEMBER]

We made bold to travell as farre as the litle Waxaw Towne,* being the first Sunday that I travell'd in all the journey, We lay att their Towne this night.

MUNDAY THE 29TH. [OF SEPTEMBER]

Haveing gott the Indians to shew us the way to the old path,† we departed from thence and travell'd till we came to a place which We called the *Persimon-Run*,‡ there growing abundance of Persimmons was the reason we called it Soe.

TUESDAY THE 30TH. [OF SEPTEMBER]

We sett out from ye Persimmon-Run, and travell'd till we att last came to the old Tradeing path that we went in, the first Journey to Carolina, where we discharged our Guns for joy that we had steer'd Soe Exact a Course, For our Aime was to come into this Path Thereabouts, We alsoe marked several Trees and writt all our names with ye date thereon, and then tooke horse and travell'd to a place that in our first [24] journey we called the *Guttling Run*,§ where we would not trouble the King and his Man to goe with us any further, But parted with him here, giveing him a Gun, powder, shott Salt, Beads, Duffill-Blanketts, and four yards of plaines, and Several other things which amounted in all to about Seaven pounds. These things We gave him on purpose that he Should goe to the *Waxaws* and gett some of them to goe with him and to marke that new discover'd roade which he faithfully sayd he would, And then we pass'd a few Indian Complements to each other and parted. That Evening We continued travelling till we came to A place called

---

* Traunter's mileages indicate that the Waxaw town was either in present-day Lancaster or Chesterfield County, about 40 miles north and east of present-day Camden, South Carolina.

† The Waxaw Road into Charleston.

‡ Written in the margin is: "Persimons being a fruit like unto Medlars." Lawson, a botanist, considered persimmons as "nearest our Medlar" (*New Voyage*, 109).

§ Guttling Creek, near present-day Camden, may have been the Wateree River, Flat Rock Creek, or Little Flat Rock Creek. Traunter also visited this place in 1698. It was near what had been Cofitachequi, now the Mulberry archaeological site just south of Camden (Beck, *Chiefdoms, Collapse*, 44).

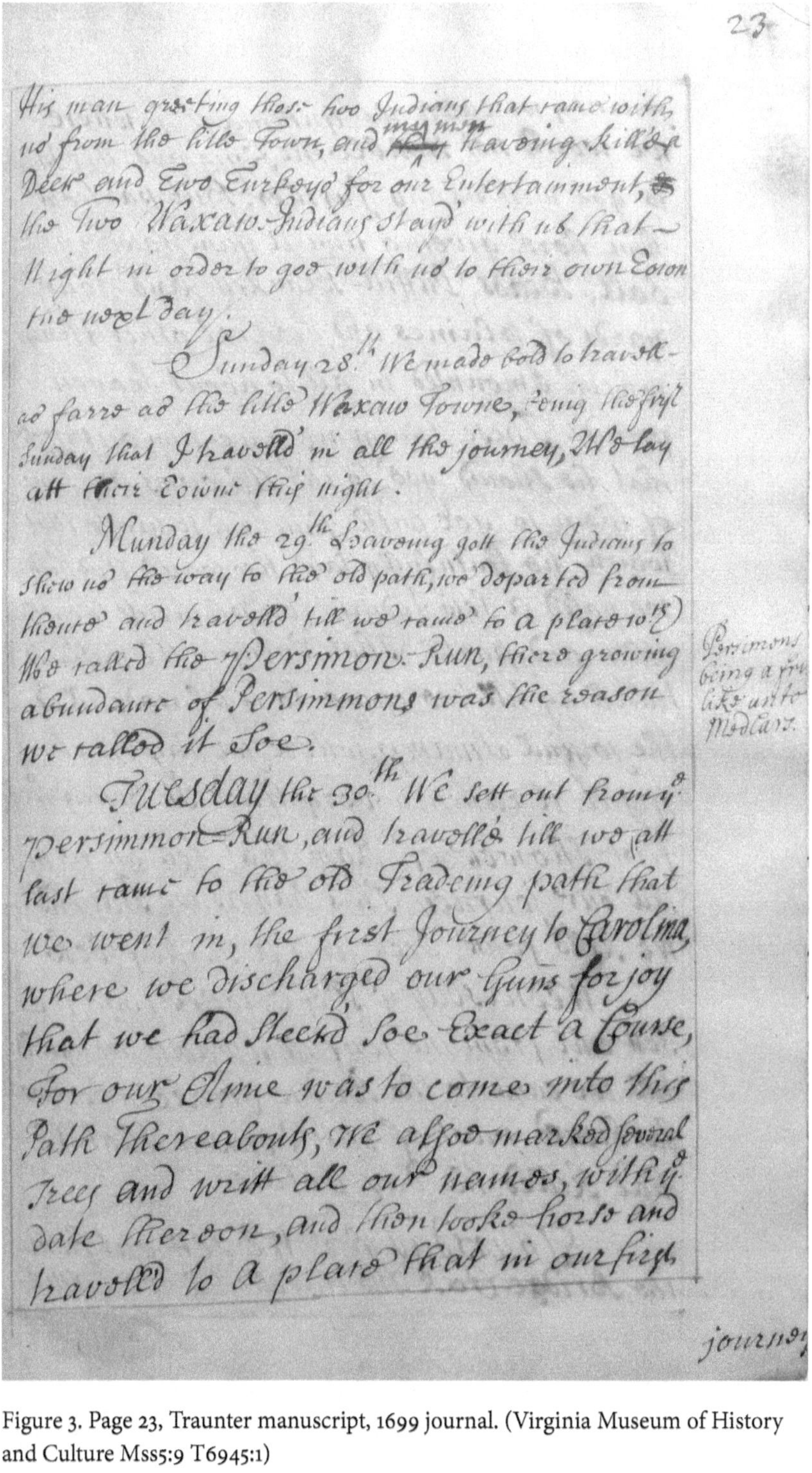

His man greeting those two Indians that came with us from the little Town, and having kill'd a Deer and two Turkeys for our Entertainment, the two Waxaw Indians stay'd with us that night in order to goe with us to their own Town the next day.

  Sunday 28.th We made bold to travell as farre as the little Waxaw Towne, being the first Sunday that I travell'd in all the journey, We lay att their Towne this night.

  Munday the 29.th Leaveing gott the Indians to show us the way to the old path, we departed from thence and travell'd till we came to a place w.ch We called the Persimon-Run, there growing abundance of Persimmons was the reason we called it soe. *Persimons being a fruit like unto Medlars*

  Tuesday the 30.th We sett out from y.e Persimon-Run, and travell'd till we att last came to the old Tradeing path that we went in, the first Journey to Carolina, where we discharged our Guns for joy that we had steer'd soe Exact a Course, For our Aime was to come into this Path thereabouts, We alsoe marked several Trees and writt all our names, with y.e date thereon, and then tooke horse and travell'd to a place that in our first journey

Figure 3. Page 23, Traunter manuscript, 1699 journal. (Virginia Museum of History and Culture Mss5:9 T6945:1)

the joyfull Swamp, where we lay that night, it raining very hard It being ye first shower of Rain that fell on us in all our journey. This Day as we Travell'd We kill'd four Deer and a Turkey Cock.

WEDNESDAY YE 1ST OF OCTOBER 1699.

We Sett out from the joyful Swamp and travell'd till we came to the Bridge Creeke* where we barbicued most of our Venison that We had killed the Day before.

THURSDAY YE 2D. [OF OCTOBER]

We sett out from the Bridge-Creek and travell'd till we came [25] to the Congree River, where we foarded over att the same Place as We did in our first journey to Carolina,† We travell'd on the other side about tenn Miles, and one of my men shott att a Bear, And I perceiveing that the Bear did not fall, I pursued him haveing a Dog with me who seiz'd the Bear, and imagining the Bear would kill my Dog, I fired and Shott my Dog & wounded the Bear, and running up towards the Bear He mett me and pursued me, Soe close that I could have noe time to load my Gunne againe, With running among the Underwood my Sword Belt broke, and as I rann, my Sword gott between my Leggs' and threw me down, and the Bear had almost Secured me, But I gott up and drew my Sword, and took to a great Oak Tree, The Bear still running round the Tree after me, and I passing at him with my Sword, but could doe noe good, Seeing that he would have tired me if I stay'd there, I rann from the Side of the Tree and Shew'd him a fair pair of Heels for it, [26] down the Hill and Soe I left him then I went to my dog haveing broke his fore-Legg up att the Shoulder, I had rather have lost any horse I had than my dog, he being an Excellent Dog for all manor of Game haveing found my Dog I was a considerable while before I could find my horse, Haveing loaded my Gunn again, I mounted and followed the Bear by his Blood, till I came into A great deep *Swamp* Soe that I could goe noe farther in pursuit of the Bear, being heartily Sorry that I had wounded my Dog and could not be revenged of the Bear, takeing my Dog up before me on horsebacke, I carried him in my Lapp

---

* Bridge Creek near modern Elgin, South Carolina.

† Traunter forded the Congaree River at the same place on both trips, probably at today's Granby Dam, and followed the same route to Charleston.

till I came up with my Company, who were Surpriz'd to See me all bloody, But when they perceived it came from the Dog their fear was qualified, thô they were all Sorry for the Dogg and persuaded me to leave him behind, which I was very unwilling to doe, But finding yt [I] could not conveniently carry him, I left him behind travelling about two Miles further my Men being before were after another Bear, the one [27] of them pursued him the other ridd round & mett him and Shott him, that he instantly dyed. He was a very large Bear but very poor, that we could not eat any of him leaveing him we travell'd about four miles and rideing up towards my Company, my Boy called to me and told me that one of my men was in pursuite of another Bear, He directed me which Way the man was gone, I putt Spurs to my horse and ridd that way but could not See him, So that I was returning againe to my Company, And walking my horse gently, I could here behind me one crying Look behind you, Look back, when looking behind me, I saw the man rideing a Gallopp and the Bear just before him, Att that I jump'd off my horse and cocked my Gunn Suffring the Bear to come within twenty foot of me, then I Scared him makeing him turne his Side to me So that I might have a full Shott att him, That as Soon as ever I turned him, I fired, and he went above a hundred paces before he lay downe and dyed, that att first I thought I had not hitt him, but goeing up to him when he was layd [28] downe, and feeling on that side that was next me when I Shott him, I made Such A hole in him that I run up my Arme to the Elbow in his Body, haveing Sixteen Swann Shott in my Gunn When I shott him, this Bear proved to be fatt Soe that we carried one half of him with us to a place called the *Savana Hutts*,* where we fared delicately, lying there that Night.

FRIDAY YE 3 D.† [OF OCTOBER]

We sett out from the *Savana Hutts* and travell'd till We came to a place within fourteene Miles of *Sante* river, haveing travell'd Soe hard that one of my horses

---

* Traunter's mileage to Savana Hutts is consistent with an archaeological site at Savany Hunt Creek, on the west side of the Congaree River south of the present-day Columbia area (Stephenson, *Basic Inventory of Archeological Sites,* 49). Lawson's map identified a "Savanna" and "Indian hutts" further south on the Santee River. Traunter called this Pond Swamp in 1698 (*Travels,* Journal One, 31).

† Traunter's mileage data between Congaree River and Santee River appears to understate the miles he traveled. Going from Bridge Creek to the Congaree River (18 miles) and then to Savana Hutts (32 miles) all on Thursday, 2 October, meant he traveled 50 miles in

tired, calling the place that we lodged att the *Tireing Branch*.* Before I Sett out, my Dog that I had wounded, came hopping on three Leggs and fawn'd upon me, he maintained his journey very well to the Settlement att Sante River, Soe that in a litle time he recover'd & was as well as ever.

SATURDAY THE 4TH. [OF OCTOBER]

We sett out from the *Tireing Branch* and travell'd till we came to Sante River,[†] being come to the other side of the River, There were some Gentlemen of my particular Acquaintance, being one Captn. James Moor, and one Captn. How,[‡] with some others. Captn. Moor and Captn. How, haveing made A Settlement on each side of the River, they being then a Surveying of their Land, haveing Survey'd All the Curious Savanaes or Meadows, together with [29] the adjacent Wood Lands att least five thousand Acres, that I doe judge it to be the best Settlement in Carolina, being to my knowledge the best Land there. We stayed att this River Severall dayes before we departed. *Sir Nathaniell Johnson* and Captn. Moor doe very much propagate the Silk Manufacture[§] haveing hitherto good Successe, That they say Carolina will be as good for making of Silk as any Countrey in the world, For that Small Quantity that was Sent to England in the vessell I came in, proved to be altogether as good as any in the World, Whilst I and my Company were here, We kill'd Soe many Turkeys that we glutted the Gentlemen that they would eat noe more, These Gentlemen were resolv'd to goe down the River in a large Boate that they had there for the use of the Plantations, on purpose to discover more good Land,

---

one day and had time for the bear hunt. His mileages from Savana Hutts to the Santee River are consistent for both journeys.

 * This is the same place Traunter called Miller's Creek in his 1698 journal (*Travels, Journal One*, 31), northeast of today's Orangeburg. Bates Mill Creek is in the vicinity of modern Fort Motte, where Lefler placed Lawson's Congaree Town (introduction to *New Voyage*, xii).

 † Traunter said Tireing Branch was within 14 miles of where he encountered Moore on the Santee River, which, according to his mileage calculations, was 11 miles north of where he crossed the Santee River in 1698 in the vicinity of modern Vance and Eutaw Springs.

 ‡ Capt. Job Howes was a Goose Creek man allied with Moore, a member of the South Carolina Commons House of Assembly (1696–1707) and its speaker from 1700 to 1705 (Sirmans, *Colonial South Carolina*, 70, 78; Salley, *JCHASC 1700*, 5).

 § Sir Nathaniel Johnson succeeded James Moore as governor of South Carolina (1703–9). Johnson established his Silk Hope plantation in South Carolina in 1689 to introduce silk manufacturing to the colony (Webber, "Nathaniel Johnson and His Son Robert," 109–10).

and to goe that way home, The River running within thirty Miles of Captn. Moor's house, Soe that I sent my people by Land with their horses and Amunition and Provision wch We had left, ordering them to goe to Captn. Moors where my horses might be taken care of, Only I kept my boy and two horses wch together with the Gentlemens horses we had appointed to meet us att the place where We were to land, when we came down the River, We discovered abundance of extraordinary good Land, there being for the most part on each Side of the River, very fine *Savanaes,* Also upon the Sand Banks that were on the River side, all the way as we Row'd notwithstanding We made a great Noise with our Oars, There were Great Flocks of [30] Turkeys that were not att all afrayd of us, I Shott att one Gang twice before they budged being very near them when I shott, and all the men in the Boate makeing a great noise, I kill'd Severall in our voyage, When landing at *Turkey Creek** our men were there before us with the horses, Soe we lay there that Night. The next Morning we took horse and Travell'd about thirty Miles to *Goose Creek,*† att which place is Captn. Moors House in *Carolina.*

An end of my Second Journey from Appomatox River in Virginia To Carolina by Land 1699.

---

* Turkey Creek is near Charleston; Traunter went there in 1698 as well.
† Goose Creek, just north of Charleston.

[31]

The names of the Places and Allso the Quantity of miles In this Seco[nd] Journey:

Munday	To Moncksneck	18
Tuesday	To Sapone Spring	27
Wednesday	To Nottoway River	24
Thursday	To Meherin River	30
Fryday	To Ronoque River	40
Munday	To Hatchers-Runn	35
Tuesday	To Napp of Reeds	26
Wednesday	To Geniton tar River	25
Thursday	To Doe Swamp	20
Fryday	To Adjusheere	10
Munday	To Haw River	20
Tuesday	To Resolute Swamp	21
Wednesday	To Diep River	20
Thursday	To Foaling Runn	19
Saterday	To Raven Runn	22
Munday	To Milky Runn	20
Tuesday	To Yadkin River	21
Wednesday	To Fishing Creek	10
Thursday	To Quarrelling Branch	20
Fryday	To Doubtfull Creek	24
Saterday	To Path Swamp	21
Sunday	To Little Waxaw Town	18
Munday	To Persimon Runn	20
Tuesday	To Joyfull Swamp	24
Wednesday	To Bridge Creek	21
Thursday	To Congree River	18
Fryday	To Savana Hutts	32
Saterday	To Tireing Branch	33
And from thence to Sante River		14
	being in all	621 [653 miles]*

} Miles

---

* Traunter's land miles add up to 653 miles, not 621 miles. He did not include the 32 miles from Congaree River to Savana Hutts and also omitted from his mileage total the approximately 120 miles he traveled on Moore's barge.

APPENDIX A
[Loughton and Traunter, Memorial to the Board of Trade, 26 July 1700]

[1] To the Right Honourable the Lords Comissioners For Trade and Plantations The Humble Memorial of Edward Loughton & Richard Tranter

Sheweth

That having discovered to one Mr Jean Couture the Encouragements we had received (with the rest of our Friends) from his Majesty for the discovery of the silver mines in Carolina,* well knowing him to be the greatest Trader and Traveller amongst the Indians for more than Twenty years, and to speak Eight or Nine several Indian Languages, we thought him a fit person to be Concerned with us as our Companion and Interpreter, and he being well satisfyed that we were realy Imployed by His Majesty in that service, he was mightily overjoyed and willingly Joyned [with]† us, and told us he was glad of this opportunity to serve his Majesty and Government; and that he would discover to us what he never Intended to have done to any, by reason the Government of Carolina had used him so Barbarously,‡ and he did intreat

---

This seventeenth-century copy was appended to Traunter's "Travels" manuscript. The original memorial by Loughton and Traunter is in the UK's National Archives, shelfmark CO 5/1260/f. 234–234v. This memorial was independently paginated in the Traunter manuscript.

* Loughton and Traunter were referencing previous testimony before the Board by their partners and the royal warrant that resulted from those appearances. These documents that preceded the silver project, and Loughton and Traunter's present testimony before the Board, are housed at the UK's National Archives: Smith and Cutler, Memorial, ff. 299–300; Board of Trade and Plantations, Representation to King William, ff. 298–299; Treasury, Warrant for John Smith and Thomas Cutler, 470.

† "With" is in the original manuscript at the UK National Archives but is missing from Traunter's copy.

‡ Loughton and Traunter delivered Jean Couture's Letter to the Board of Trade, the original of which is in the UK's National Archives; see Couture, Letter, f. 236. A seventeenth-

and Importune us to take this Voyage, which we have purposely done having no other business in England, but to bring his Letter to yor Lordships, and Humbly to Lay before this Honourable [2] Board what farther the said Jean Couture did desire & request of us to doe which was, that he with three others in Company did Travel through several Nations of Indians above a hundred Leagues beyond ye Appalletean Mountains where he verily believes that no Europeans had ever been before, that he the said Couture did pick up from a Small Rivulet falling from the Rocks amongst the sands and Stones, about foure pounds wheight of fine Gold in Small Grains of Different bigness; and that there were great quantityes of Very small dust mixt with the Sands, which he did not take up but only the bigest Grains that were Clean from Sand, and that there were very many Blew Stones about that place which he verily believes were Lapis Lazuly,* and that this was not far from a Branch of a Navigable River. And hee farther saith that he Received from a Nation of Indians Inhabiting by a Very great Lake as Many Pearls as both his hands Could Contain of Different sizes and some of a Good oriental Colour, and does believe the greatest part would be so if they were rightly taken from the shell fish without broyling them, as the manner of those Indians is to do, more for the sake of the Fish than the Value of the Pearl. That as soon as he came so far back to be within the Limits and bounds of the Indian Traders [3] the Indian that Carryed his box, wherein was his dividend of about a pound of the Gold, together with his pearles run away from him; and not Long after his three Companions were all murdered by the Indians, and he narrowly Escapt by understanding their Language. That he verily believes this was done by the Instigation of some of the Indian Traders for the sake of their Gold, and to Compell them to discover where they had it; because that when he came to Charles Town he was Imprisoned by the Governor,† without

---

century copy of Couture's letter was appended to Traunter's "Travels" manuscript; see appendix D in this work.

* Bluestones, perhaps even blue slate. Lawson found bluestones at Uwharrie River that he said made good millstones (*New Voyage*, 56). Lapis lazuli is not found in the Viriginia-Carolina piedmont.

† Joseph Blake was then governor of South Carolina. He was a landgrave and twice served as governor of South Carolina between 1694 and 1700, except for the time that his uncle, Proprietor John Archdale, held that office (1695–96) (Sirmans, *Colonial South Carolina*, 56). Couture's claim is consistent with those of "Great Numbers" of men who had been "unjustly imprissoned" on "Pretended" warrants, beaten, and subject to "Divers abuses" (Salley, *JCHASC 1700*, 15–21). The man accused of falsely jailing the men was Robert Daniels (Daniells), an ally of James Moore (Edgar, *South Carolina*, 93).

any other known Cause, and this he the raither believes, because they were very pressing to know whether he had not discovered some great riches in his Travells, but neither by Threats, nor Intreaties would he discover any thing to them. And finding they Could work no Effect on him they at Last releast him after a hundred pound Charge to him.

That the said Couture humbly prays to be Enabled securely to go to that place, without danger or molestation at his return, and only desires for recompence what he Can bring from thence at once That the said Jean Couture is bound to us and three others in 500li Bond, and we all by Oath to each other, to goe immediately on our Return to Carolina accompanied with such Indians and Servants we shall have occasion For to the place where the Gold was taken up, as also the silver oar already promised

That Should his Majesty give us a Reward of Five Thousand pounds to undertake this design [4] We could not accomplish it unless yor Lordships are pleased to think it reasonable we should have some Warrant or Authority* to secure and Indemnify us, And those we shall have occasion to make use of for the furtherance of his Majesties Service in this affair, against all opposers otherwise tis absolutely imposible for us to do His Majesty any Service herein.

That if it shall be thought fit to Grant such warrant to us together with Mr Jean Couture, Mr John Smith Mr David Maybank & Mr Solomon Legare and Henry Netherton,† we are willing to Venture our Lives in this Service, and to bring his Majesty a Satisfactory proof of the Truth thereof, and only desire what your Lordships in your great Wisdomes shall think sufficient to bear our Expenses (and according to the Custom of those Countryes) to make presents to the Indians, thro those Nations we shall pass of such things they Esteem, as Guns Powder & Shot Looking glasses, Bells, paint, and many other things too Tedious to trouble yor Lordships with all, that they delight in

All which is most humbly submitted to yor Lordships Consideration by
Edward Loughton
& Richd Tranter

---

* Traunter already had a royal license, the authority of which Moore and others in Charleston refused to recognize, so this request was a political statement (Dahlberg, "To the common Good," 337).

† Henry Netherton was briefly in South Carolina before he returned to Virginia, allegedly without settling all the debts he incurred in Charleston (Moore, Letter to Thomas Cutler, 25 December 1700, f. 331–331v). See also Tucker, *Colonial Virginians*, 39, 43; and Fothergill, *Wills of Westmoreland County*, 62.

APPENDIX B
[Smith, Memorial to the Board of Trade, 26 July 1700.]

[1] To the Right Honourable the Lords Commissioners For Trade and Plantations The Humble Memorial of John Smith

Sheweth

That by one Memorial given your Lordships the 17th June 1699, your Lordships were then Informed what had been done toward the discovery of the silver mines in Carolina,* and what farther at this time we can Informe yor Lordships is: that Mr Good with his friends there did according to their Intention in the Memorial given your Lordships set forward on their Journey towards the mines, as far as the Savana Town, about 170 miles from Charles Town,† where Mr Good on some search amongst the Rocks did unfortunately Loose his Life by a fall into the Water and was taken up Dead from between the Rocks, very much Bruised the 27th May 1699, and by his Death his Relations of Broad Chalk in the County of Wilts‡ have Lost a Second Life in

---

When this memorial was presented to the Board of Trade, John Smith (c. 1655–1723) was a member of Parliament, chancellor of the exchequer, and a former member of King William III's Privy Council. He served as Speaker of the English House of Commons from 1705 to 1708 and was elected the first speaker of Great Britain's House of Commons after England's unification with Scotland. The original copy of Smith's memorial is in the UK's National Archives, shelfmark CO 5/1260/f. 232–232v. A reference to Smith's memorial appears in the Board of Trade's Minute Book for 1700, 128–29. It is the second document appended to Traunter's "Travels" manuscript.

* Board of Trade and Plantations, Minutes, 1699, 77.

† This is probably a reference to the place Traunter called Savana Hutts, which was 164 miles north from Charleston, and not the Shawnee town north and west of Charleston. Lawson's 1709 map also shows a Savana Town on the Santee/Congaree River.

‡ William Good was from Broad Chalke, Wiltshire, part of the estates owned by Thomas Herbert, the 8th Earl of Pembroke. Pembroke backed the silver project. See Randolph, Letter to Bridgewater, ff. 77–79.

APPENDIX B

an Estate of £100 per Annum, being Tennants to his Excellency the Right Honourable the Earl of Pembrook,* & the so great Lose to his Friends depended on his Life, yet Such was his Zeale for his Majesties Service and his Confidence of success in this matter (if death had not prevented) that t'was as well his Friends [2] as his own desire to goe on that undertaking. That his unfortunate Death put a Stop to their farther proceeding, having but one Companion with them their Indian Hunter running away from them and was disappointed of an other Indian Hunter and Interpreter Called Indian Ben, on whom they much depended, and that Mr Loughton Lost a month's Time in Fruitless Endeavors to procure Him to go to the Savana Town with him to his Friends, who Stayd there on purpose for him that they veryly believe they were prevented from having him by Captn Moor, whose Letter of the 3d of April 1699 was Laid before your Lordships,† though We Cannot believe he had any honest Intention for his Majesties Service (not withstanding what he saith there) by his refusing to subscribe his Name to it, And by what appears since tis Evident he has done great prejudice to his Majestie's Service as much as in him Lay; For tho his Request was fully answered by sending the Person to him that was presented to your Lordships the 27th of September Last, being one well skilled in the Refinning & Seperating Silver from the Oar,‡ yet he has done nothing with him but Triffled away time with promises that he would Set forward his Journey the beginning of Aprill [3] Last and has kept that person in suspence from January the time of his arrival there till may last, and then told him that he would neither goe with him nor allow him any thing for the Lose of his time althô it was his own Voluntary promise to the Contrary.

These misfortunes together with the Discourgm:ts from Governors Pro-

---

* Thomas Herbert, the 8th Earl of Pembroke, Privy Counsellor, Lord Lieutenant of Wiltshire, MP for Wilton, and a former president of the Royal Society (1689–90).

† Moore wrote nearly identical letters to Edward Randolph and Thomas Cutler, both of which were read at the Board of Trade on 19 June 1699: Moore, Letter to Randolph, 1 March 1699, ff. 75–76; Moore, Letter to Cutler, 3 April 1699, ff. 82–83. See also Board of Trade, Minute Book, 1699, 77–78. Moore claimed he discovered silver mines in 1690 (1691 in the letter to Cutler) but suppressed this information for fear that "the Report of a Silver Mine among us would incite and encourage the French in America if not in Europe to invade us." Moore also referenced Montagu's role in the letter to Edward Randolph (referenced above).

‡ On 27 September 1699 Smith and Cutler addressed the Board of Trade about Moore's mineral claims (in letters cited in preceding fn). The Board allowed Smith to independently send the refiner Moore requested (Board of Trade, Minute Book, 1699, 191–92).

prietors,* and those in their Interest as Captn Moore &c, who now know the designe, and as tis believed doe all they can to hinder his Majesties Service herein Therefor tis humbly presumed that t'will be Impossible this undertaking should succeed without the undertakers can have sufficient warrant and Authority to Indemnify and secure them from the Violence of their Government at Carolina, who threaten to Imprison them, and have Actually Imprisioned Some already & put them to great Charge and trouble before they could be releast. This will be Evidenced to yor Lordships by two persons of Good Credit and Reputation Concerned in this affair, the one Edward Loughton, the Other Richd Traunter, Loughton having more than a hundred pounds per annum, in Charles Town and Lost as much more by the fire,† The other has been one of the Greatest Travellers amongst the Indians‡ & Speaks several of their Languages, and has Traded as Store keeper & Factor amongst them for five and twenty hundred pounds per annum for [4] several years, and can be here well recommended to yor Lordships.

I hope it will not seem Strange to yor Lordships that Attempts of this Nature at so great distance should at first be Lyable to many Contingencies and disappointments; that Cannot possibly be foreseen, Especialy when we were to Cope with an Interest seperate from his Majesties, and therefore this Lose of time there being a whole year Lost by Captn Moors unfair dealing and fals promises are such disappoimts with Expence of Money that could not be fore seen nor be prevented by us.

That Whereas His Majesty was gratiously pleased to allow Six hundred pounds to Three persons,§ as we presume will Appear to yor Lordships by Mr Secretary Vernons¶ Letter to your Lordships and to the Lords of the Treasury,

---

* South Carolina governors were appointed by the Lords Proprietors of Carolina, whose authority was independent of the Board of Trade.

† On 1 February 1698 a fire destroyed one third of Charleston (Navin, *Grim Years*, 134).

‡ Smith conflated or confused some of Traunter's attributes with those of Couture. Loughton and Traunter used nearly identical language in their memorial to describe Couture.

§ The Treasury Warrant advanced £600 for the silver mine project, but only £400 was dispersed. Smith was requesting that his partners be given the remaining £200 (Board of Trade, Minute Book, 1698, 60; Treasury, Warrant for John Smith and Thomas Cutler, f. 470).

¶ James Vernon, William III's secretary of state and secretary of his Privy Council, presented the project for King William's approval and funding (Board of Trade, Minute Book, 1698, 60; Treasury, Warrant for John Smith and Thomas Cutler, f. 470).

APPENDIX B

and that only Foure hundred pounds has been Received, I humbly pray that if your Lordships should not think fit to give any farther Incouragement yet that you would please to favour Loughton and Tranter, with the remaining Two hundred pounds, to buy Indian Trading Goods to present the Indians with all, which I believe they would be well Contented with, and of what Consequence the possession of such Treasure as is set forth in their [5] Memorial, would be to any other power (there being Two French men Amongst them & one of them a Goldsmith and Jeweller)* is Humbly Submitted

To yor Lordships great Wisdome
John Smith

---

* Both Jean Couture and Solomon Legaré were Frenchmen; Legaré was a silversmith/goldsmith.

APPENDIX C
An Abstract of the Proceedings relating to the Discovery of Silver Mines in Carolina.

[1] Mr. Good and Cutler, the Two persons to whome this matter was related, arived at Charles Town in Carolina December ye 4th 1698—as soon as the season permitted, which was the beginning of May 1699, Good with his Friends there set out on their journey, with Indian Servants, and at a place called the Savana Falls about 170 miles from Charles Town,* Good was unfortunately killed, by a fall from the Rocks, and their Indian Guide and Interpreter & their Hunter ran away from them, and they were by these Accidents forc't to returne back to Charles Town, and the designe we had to have kept this Affair secret, as we were Commanded by his Majestie to doe, till ye proof was made, was quite frustrated, by the Governments there knowing of it, who doe all they can to oppose such discoverys, & would know by what Authority they Acted, & threatened to call them to Acco:t if they made any further attempts. In the mean time whilst Good & his Friends was gone on the discovery, Cutler ye better to Strengthen the report made, and that we might have Two strings to our Bow, came over to England in June 1699 with a farther [2] Information from one Capt. Moor, to the Lords Com:ers of Trade,† That he the said Moor had taken up seven several pieces of Oar with his own hands at seven several places, that he sent them by an Ingenious Friend to be Tryd in London, that Two of the seven proved very rich, and one Indifferent good,

---

This appears to be an original manuscript. No version of it exists in the National Archives. It may be a draft of Smith's memorial or a private record. It was written on smaller paper, 7.25 by 11.63 inches, and was folded to make two leaves. It appears to have been separately inserted into the quire of documents before all were bound together by Mellon.

* Smith's Savana Falls was probably near Traunter's Savana Hutts, on present-day Savany Hunt Creek.

† Smith was referencing Moore's letter to Randolph (1 March 1699) and Moore's letter to Cutler (3 April 1699) (Moore, Letter to Edward Randolph, ff. 75–76; Moore, Letter to Thomas Cutler, ff. 82–83).

and he only desired we might send him a man that was skill'd in Smelting & Refining & he would doe ye rest him self. we accordingly sent him a Smelter & Refiner by the next shipp yt went which arrived there December 1699. This Capt. Moor pretended till April 1700 that he would goe with the man on the Expedition, & at last positively refused it & as we suppose he being a man Interested in that Government, did this on purpose to ruine this undertaking by delays That the others Concerned in this Affair, seeing how great prejudice this Moor had done to his Majesties Service, they saw there was no way left but to Come over to procure something that might Inable them to proceed, Loughton and Traunter coming here for that purpose & to bring Mr Jean Coutures discoverys. This is the whole Truth of the proceedings heitherto, as will be Evidenced by Mr Loughton & Mr Traunter.

    John Smith

APPENDIX D
[Jean Couture, Letter read at the Board of Trade, 26 July 1700]

[1] Charles Town March the 22th 1699/10*
To the kings most Excellent Majesty or the Right Honourable the Lords Comm:ers for Trade and Plantations

Having the opportunity to be in Company with one Mr William Good, and Mr David Maybanck, at the Savana Town† in may last and Entering in discource, I understood where they were bound in your Majesties Service, In which Mr Good was unfortunately dround, I had assisted them else had he Lived, where your Majesty should have had good satisfaction. for I have taken up four pound wheight of Gold with my own hands, but just as I Came within the Limits of the Indian Traders (my Indian that carryd my box wherein was about a pound of Gold & as many pearl as I Could hold in both my hands ran away from me) by the Ill advice of the Traders that they might take from him what he had of mine so that I never heard of any of my things again, When I came to Charles Town the Governor put me in Prison, but for what I know not, neither did he but upon suspicion that I had discovered some great riches in my Travels, but finding yt I would not discover any the Least triffle of my busyness, they released me;‡ nevertheless they made me pay for my

---

Traunter and Loughton delivered this letter to the Board of Trade in July 1700. The original is held at the UK's National Archives, shelfmark CO 5/1260/f. 236. The Couture letter appended to Traunter's "Travels" manuscript is on a single piece of paper, written on both sides, that is larger (7.63 by 12.25 inches) than Smith's Abstract.

  * 22 March 1700.
  † Couture did not travel with Good and Maybank from Charleston but met them in the vicinity of present-day Columbia, South Carolina.
  ‡ Joseph Blake was the governor of South Carolina Province in 1699. Couture was not alone in his imprisonment; several men made similar claims to South Carolina's Commons House of Assembly (Salley, *JCHASC 1700*, 15–21).

APPENDIX D

obstinacy, Imposing such Charges upon me that it Cost one hundred pounds befor I got out. I do much suspect that they had my Box by [2] reason they were so urgent with me to know of my discoveries, that had I not seen an order from your Majesty with Mr Good and Maybank, at the Savana Town I had not discovered it to any If your Majesty be pleased to grant an Order from under your Sacred Majestie's hand that we be not molested, I have obliged my self to go with the bearer Mr Loughton, Mr Maybank, Mr Legare & any one person that they shall think Capable of such an undertaking, to the place where I took up the foresaid Gold, Mr Loughton will give your Majesty further satisfaction, No more at present from your true and ever
  Loyal Servant & Subject
  Jean Couture[*]

---

[*] The document is written in two hands: one person wrote the body of the document; the signature is more labored.

Bibliography

Adams, Lars C. "'Sundry Murders and Depredations': A Closer Look at the Chowan War, 1676–1677." *North Carolina Historical Review* 90, no. 2 (April 2013): 149–72.

Adams, Natalie, and Michael Trinkley. [1992]. "Archaeological Reconnaissance and Survey of the Granby River Front Tract, Richland County, South Carolina." Columbia, SC: Chicora Foundation, 2001. https://dc.statelibrary.sc.gov/handle/10827/33364.

Adams, Percy G. *Travelers and Travel Liars: 1660–1800*. New York: Dover, 1980.

Allen, John Logan. *North American Exploration*. Vol. 2, *A Continent Defined*. Lincoln: University of Nebraska Press, 1997.

Alvord, Charles Walworth, and Lee Bidgood, eds. *The First Explorations of the Trans-Allegheny Region by the Virginians, 1650–1674*. Cleveland: Arthur H. Clark, 1912.

Appelbaum, Robert, and John Wood Sweet, eds. *Envisioning an English Empire: Jamestown and the Making of the North Atlantic World*. Philadelphia: University of Pennsylvania Press, 2005.

Armitage, David, and Michael J. Braddick, eds. *The British Atlantic World, 1500–1800*. 2nd ed. New York: Palgrave, 2009.

Ashe, Thomas. "Carolina, or a Description of the Present State of that Country." In *Narratives of Early Carolina, 1650–1708*, edited by Alexander S. Salley Jr, 135–59. New York: Barnes and Noble, 1953 [1911].

Axtell, James. *The Indians' New South: Cultural Change in the Colonial Southeast*. Baton Rouge: Louisiana State University Press, 1997.

———. *Natives and Newcomers: The Cultural Origins of North America*. New York: Oxford University Press, 2001.

Barnett, Louise K. *The Ignoble Savage: American Literary Racism, 1790–1890*. Westport, CT: Greenwood Press, 1975.

Barr, Daniel P. *Unconquered: The Iroquois League at War in Colonial America*. Westport, CT: Praeger, 2006.

Barr, Juliana, and Edward Countryman, eds. *Contested Spaces of Early America*. Philadelphia: University of Pennsylvania Press, 2014.

Bates, Susan Baldwin, and Harriott Cheves Leland, eds. *Proprietary Records of South*

Carolina. Vol. 1, *Abstracts of Records of the Secretary of the Province, 1675–1695*. Charleston, SC: History Press, 2005.

Bauer, Ralph. *The Cultural Geography of Colonia American Literatures: Empire, Travel, Modernity.* New York: Cambridge University Press, 2003.

Baxter, Stephen B. *The Development of the Treasury, 1600–1702.* Cambridge, MA: Harvard University Press, 1957.

Beck, Robin. *Chiefdoms, Collapse, and Coalescence in the Early American South.* New York: Cambridge University Press, 2013.

Beck, Robin A., Christopher B. Rodning, and David G. Moore, eds. *Fort San Juan and the Limits of Empire: Colonialism and Household Practice at the Berry Site.* Gainesville: University Press of Florida, 2016.

Berkhofer, Robert F., Jr. *The White Man's Indian: Images of the American Indian from Columbus to the Present.* New York: Alfred A. Knopf, 1978.

Berland, Kevin, ed. *The Dividing Line Histories of William Byrd II of Westover.* Chapel Hill: Omohundro Institute of Early American History and Culture / University of North Carolina Press, 2013.

Berland, Kevin, Jan Kirsten Gilliam, and Kenneth A. Lockridge, eds. *The Commonplace Book of William Byrd II of Westover.* Chapel Hill: Omohundro Institute of Early American History and Culture / University of North Carolina Press, 2001.

Beverley, Robert. *The History and Present State of Virginia: A New Edition.* Edited with an introduction by Susan Scott Parrish. Chapel Hill: Omohundro Institute of Early American Literature and Culture / University of North Carolina Press, 2018.

Billings, Warren M., ed. *The Old Dominion in the Seventeenth Century: A Documentary History of Virginia, 1606–1700.* Rev. ed. Chapel Hill: Omohundro Institute of Early American History and Culture / University of North Carolina Press, 2007.

Bland, Edward. *Discovery of New Brittaine.* In *The First Explorations of the Trans-Allegheny Region by the Virginians, 1650–1674*, edited by Charles Walworth Alvord and Lee Bidgood, 105–30. Cleveland: Arthur H. Clark, 1912.

Board of Trade and Plantations. Representation to King William III. 18 April 1698. CO 391/11/f. 60. National Archives, Kew, Surrey, UK.

———. Minute Book. 1698. CO 391/11. National Archives, Kew, Surrey, UK.

———. Minute Book. 1699. CO 391/12. National Archives, Kew, Surrey, UK.

———. Minute Book. 1700. CO 391/13. National Archives, Kew, Surrey, UK.

Boudreaux, Edmond A. *The Archaeology of Town Creek.* Tuscaloosa: University of Alabama Press, 2007.

———. "A Mississippian's Ceramic Chronology for the Town Creek Region." *North Carolina Archaeology* 56 (Oct 2007): 1–57.

Boudreaux, Edmond A. III, Maureen Meyers, and Jay K. Johnson, eds. *Contact, Colonialism, and Native Communities in the Southeastern United States.* Gainesville: University of Florida Press, 2020.

Bowne, Eric E. "'Bold and Warlike People': The Basis of Westo Power." In *Light on the Path:*

The Anthropology and History of the Southeastern Indians, edited by Thomas J. Pluckhahn and Robbie Ethridge, 123–32. Tuscaloosa: University of Alabama Press, 2006.

———. "Dr. Henry Woodward's Role in Early Carolina Indian Relations." In *Creating and Contesting Carolina: Proprietary Era Histories*, edited by Michelle LeMaster and Bradford J. Wood, 73–94. Columbia: University of South Carolina Press, 2013.

———. *The Westo Indians: Slave Traders of the Early Colonial South*. Tuscaloosa: University of Alabama Press, 2005.

Boyd, William K., ed. *William Byrd's Histories of the Dividing Line Betwixt Virginia and North Carolina*. New York: Dover, 1967.

Braund, Kathryn E. Holland. *Deerskins and Duffels: The Creek Indian Trade with Anglo-America, 1685–1815*. 2nd ed. Lincoln: University of Nebraska Press, 2008.

Briceland, Alan Vance. "British Exploration of the United States Interior." In *North American Exploration*, vol. 2, *A Continent Defined*, edited by John Logan Allen, 269–327. Lincoln: University of Nebraska Press, 1997.

———. "'It has been long our policy to preserve these neighboring Indians and yet to avoid open breach with the Senecas': 1677–1722." Unpublished chapter (19) from *Westward from Virginia*.

———. Phone conversation with the editor, 10 July 2019.

———. *Westward from Virginia: The Exploration of the Virginia-Carolina Frontier, 1650–1710*. Charlottesville: University Press of Virginia, 1987.

Brose, David S., C. Wesley Cowan, and Robert C. Mainfort Jr., eds. *Societies in Eclipse: Archaeology of the Eastern Woodlands Indians, A.D. 1400–1700*. Tuscaloosa: University of Alabama Press, 2001.

Brown, Philip. "Early Indian Trade in the Development of South Carolina: Politics, Economics, and Social Mobility during the Proprietary Period, 1670–1719." *South Carolina Historical Magazine* 76 (April 1975): 118–28.

Brückner, Martin, ed. *Early American Cartographies*. Chapel Hill, NC: Omohundro Institute of Early American History and Culture, 2011.

Byrd, William II. *Prose Works of William Byrd of Westover: Narratives of a Colonial Virginian*. Edited by Louis B. Wright. Cambridge, MA: Harvard University Press, 1966.

Cabeza de Vaca, Álvar Núñez. *The Account: Álvar Núñez Cabeza de Vaca's Relación*. Edited and translated by Martin A. Favata and José B. Fernández. Houston: Arte Público Press, 1993.

Calcaterra, Angela. *Literary Indians: Aesthetics and Encounter in American Literature to 1920*. Chapel Hill: University of North Carolina Press, 2018.

Cameron, Catherine M., Paul Kelton, and Alan C. Swedlund, eds. *Beyond Germs: Native Depopulation in North America*. Tucson: University of Arizona Press, 2015.

Carey, Daniel. "Compiling Nature's History: Travellers and Travel Narratives in the Early Royal Society." *Annals of Science* 54 (1997): 269–92.

Carson, James Taylor. "American Historians and Indians." *Historical Journal* 49, no. 3 (2006): 921–33.

———. *Making an Atlantic World: Circles, Paths, and Stories from the Colonial Southeast*. Knoxville: University of Tennessee Press, 2007.

Castillo, Susan, and Ivy Schweitzer, eds. *The Literatures of Colonial America: An Anthology*. Malden, MA: Blackwell, 2001.

Catesby, Mark. *The Natural History of Carolina, Florida and the Bahama Islands*. 2 vols. London, 1743.

Champagne, Duane. "Centering Indigenous Nations within Indigenous Methodologies." *Wicazo Sa Review* 30, no. 1 (Spring 2015): 57–81.

Cheney, C. R., ed. *Handbook of Dates for Students of English History*. London: Royal Historical Society / University College London, 1970.

Coe, Joffre Lanning. *Town Creek Indian Mound: A Native American Legacy*. Chapel Hill: University of North Carolina Press, 1995.

Collet, John. *A Compleat Map of North Carolina from an Actual Survey*. 1770. K. Top.122.51.2. TAB. British Library, London, UK.

———. *A Map of the Southern Part of North Carolina*. 1768. K. Top.122.50. British Library, London, UK.

Cooper, Thomas, ed. *The Statutes at Large of South Carolina, 1682–1716*. Vol. 2. Columbia, SC: A. S. Johnston, 1837.

Couture, Jean. Letter [to the Board of Trade, ca. 1700]. CO 5/1260/f. 236. National Archives, Kew, Surrey, UK.

Crane, Verner W. *The Southern Frontier, 1670–1732*. Tuscaloosa: University of Alabama Press, 2004.

———. "The Tennessee River as the Road to Carolina: The Beginnings of Exploration and Trade." *Mississippi Valley Historical Review* 3, no. 1 (June 1916): 3–18.

Crittenden, Charles Christopher. "Overland Travel and Transportation in North Carolina, 1763–1789." *North Carolina Historical Review* 8, no. 3 (1931): 239–57.

Cutler, Thomas. Memorial of Thomas Cutler. 19 June 1699. CO 5/1258/f. 80. National Archives, Kew, Surrey, UK.

Dahlberg, Sandra L. "'To the common Good of my Country': 'The Travels of Richard Traunter' and the Carolina Silver Project." *Early American Studies* 17, no. 3 (Summer 2019): 315–42.

Daniel, I. Randolph, Jr., and J. Robert Butler. "An Archaeological Survey and Petrographic Description of Rhyolite Sources in the Uwharrie Mountains, North Carolina." *Southern Indian Studies* 45 (1996): 1–37.

Daniels, Christine, and Michael V. Kennedy, eds. *Negotiated Empires: Centers and Peripheries in the Americas, 1500–1820*. New York: Routledge, 2002.

Davis, R. P. Stephen, Jr. "Cultural Landscape of the North Carolina Piedmont at Contact." In *Transformation of the Southeastern Indians, 1540–1760*, edited by Robbie Ethridge and Charles Hudson, 135–54. Jackson: University Press of Mississippi, 2002.

———. "The Travels of James Needham and Gabriel Arthur through Virginia, North Carolina, and Beyond, 1673–1674." *Southern Indian Studies* 39 (Oct. 1990): 31–55.

Davis, R. P. Stephen, Jr., and H. Trawick Ward. "The Evolution of Siouan Communities in Piedmont North Carolina." *Southeastern Archaeology* 40, no. 1 (Summer 1991): 40–53.
De Krey, Gary Stuart. *A Fractured Society: The Politics of London in the First Age of Party, 1688–1715.* New York: Oxford University Press, 1985.
Deloria, Philip J., and Neal Salisbury, eds. *A Companion to American Indian History.* Malden, MA: Blackwell, 2004.
Dickens, Roy S., Jr., H. Trawick Ward, and R. P. Stephen Davis Jr., eds. *The Siouan Project: Seasons 1 and II.* Chapel Hill: University of North Carolina, 1987.
Dobbs, G. Rebecca. "Frontier Settlement Development and 'Initial Conditions': The Case of the North Carolina Piedmont and the Indian Trading Path." *Historical Geography* 37 (2009): 114–37.
Dobyns, Henry F. *Their Number Become Thinned: Native American Population Dynamics in Eastern North America.* Knoxville: University of Tennessee Press, 1983.
Dryden, John. *Aureng-Zebe, or The Great Mogul* [1675]. In *John Dryden: Three Plays*, edited by George Saintsbury, 265–355. New York: Hill and Wang, 1968.
Dudley, Paul. "An Account of the Rattlesnake." *Philosophical Transactions of the Royal Society of London* 32, no. 376 (1723): 292–95.
Dunbar-Ortiz, Roxanne. *An Indigenous Peoples' History of the United States.* Boston: Beacon Press, 2014.
Edelson, S. Max. *Plantation Enterprise in Colonial South Carolina.* Cambridge, MA: Harvard University Press, 2006.
Edgar, Walter. *South Carolina: A History.* Columbia: University of South Carolina Press, 1998.
Ethridge, Robbie. "Creating the Shatter Zone: Indian Slave Traders and the Collapse of the Southeastern Chiefdoms." In *Light on the Path: The Anthropology and History of the Southeastern Indians*, edited by Thomas J. Pluckhahn and Robbie Ethridge, 207–18. Tuscaloosa: University of Alabama Press, 2006.
———. *From Chicaza to Chickasaw: The European Invasion and the Transformation of the Mississippian World, 1540–1715.* Chapel Hill: University of North Carolina Press, 2010.
———. "Navigating the Mississippian World: Infrastructure in the Sixteenth-Century Native South." In *Forging Southeastern Identities: Social Archaeology, Ethnohistory, and Folklore of the Mississippian to Early Historic South.* Edited by Gregory A. Waselkov and Marvin T. Smith, 62–84. Tuscaloosa: University of Alabama Press, 2017.
Ethridge, Robbie, and Charles Hudson, eds. *Transformation of the Southeastern Indians, 1540–1760.* Jackson: University Press of Mississippi, 2002.
Ethridge, Robbie, and Jeffery M. Mitchem. "The Interior South at the Time of Spanish Exploration." In *Native and Spanish New Worlds: Sixteenth-Century Entradas in the American Southwest and Southeast*, edited by Clay Mathers, Jeffrey M. Mitchem, and Charles M. Haecker, 170–88. Tucson: University of Arizona Press, 2013.

Everett, C. S. "'They shalbe slaves for their lives': Indian Slavery in Colonial Virginia." In *Indian Slavery in Colonial America,* edited by Alan Gallay, 67–108. Lincoln: University of Nebraska Press, 2009.

Fecher, Rebecca Taft. "The Trading Path and North Carolina." *Journal of Backcountry Studies* 3, no. 2 (2008): 1–13.

Feeley, Stephen. "Intercolonial Conflict and Cooperation during the Tuscarora War." In *New Voyages to Carolina: Reinterpreting North Carolina History,* eds. Larry E. Tise and Jeffrey J. Crow, 60–84. Chapel Hill: University of North Carolina Press, 2017.

Field, Ophelia. *The Kit-Cat Club.* London: Harper, 2009.

Fitts, Mary Elizabeth. "Mapping Catawba Coalescence." *North Carolina Archaeology* 55 (2006): 1–59.

Floyd, Viola C. *Lancaster County, South Carolina: Tours.* Lancaster, SC: Lancaster County Historical Commission, 1956.

Fogelson, Raymond D., ed. *Handbook of North American Indians.* Vol. 14, *The Southeast.* Washington, DC: Smithsonian Institute, 2004.

Foley, Nora K., and Robert A. Ayuso. "Gold Deposits of the Carolina Slate Belt, Southeastern United States—Age and Origin of the Major Gold Producers: U.S. Geological Survey Open Report 2012–1179." U.S. Geological Survey. https://pubs.usgs.gov /of/2012/1179/pdf/ofr2012-1179.pdf.

Fothergill, Augusta B. *Wills of Westmoreland County, Virginia: 1654–1800.* Richmond, VA: Appeals Press, 1925.

Fry, Joshua, and Peter Jefferson. *A Map of the Most Inhabited Part of Virginia Containing the Whole Province of Maryland: With Part of Pensilvania, New Jersey and North Carolina.* London, 1755. Map F221 1755:3. Virginia Museum of History and Culture, Richmond.

Gallay, Alan, ed. *Indian Slavery in Colonial America.* Lincoln: University of Nebraska Press, 2009.

———. *The Indian Slave Trade: The Rise of the English Empire in the American South, 1670–1717.* New Haven, CT: Yale University Press, 2002.

Galloway, Patricia. *Choctaw Genesis, 1500–1700.* Lincoln: University of Nebraska Press, 1995.

Gascoigne, John. "The Royal Society, Natural History and the Peoples of the 'New World(s)', 1660–1800." *British Journal for the History of Science* 42, no. 4 (2009): 539–62.

Good, Henry. Will of Henry Good. 13 January 1686. P2/G/367. Wiltshire and Swindon History Centre, Chippenham, Wiltshire, UK.

Good, Jane. Will of Jane Good. 1 June 1702. P2/G/620. Wiltshire and Swindon History Centre, Chippenham, Wiltshire, UK.

Greene, Jack P., Rosemary Brana-Shute, and Randy J. Sparks, eds. *Money, Trade, and Power: The Evolution of Colonial South Carolina's Plantation Society.* Columbia: University of South Carolina Press, 2001.

Guasco, Michael. "To 'Doe Some Good Upon Their Countrymen': The Paradox of Indian Slavery in Early Anglo-America." *Journal of Social History* 41, no. 2 (2007): 389–411.

Hall, Joseph M., Jr. *Zamumo's Gifts: Indian-European Exchange in the Colonial Southeast*. Philadelphia: University of Pennsylvania Press, 2009.

Hammett, Julia E. "Ethnohistory of Aboriginal Landscapes in the Southeastern United States." *Southern Indian Studies* 41 (1992): 1–50.

Hanna, Mark G. "Protecting the Rights of Englishmen: The Rise and Fall of Carolina's Piratical State." In *Creating and Contesting Carolina: Proprietary Era Histories*, edited by Michelle LeMaster and Bradford J. Wood, 295–318. Columbia: University of South Carolina Press, 2013.

Hariot, Thomas. *A Briefe and True Report*. In *Captain John Smith: Writings with Other Narratives of Roanoke, Jamestown, and the First English Settlement of America*, edited by James Horn. New York: Library of America, 2007. 874–905.

Hening, William Waller, ed. *The Statutes at Large; Being a Collection of All the Laws of Virginia, From the First Session of the Legislature, In the Year 1619*. Richmond, VA: Franklin Press, 1819.

Hodge, Frederick Webb. *Handbook of the American Indians North of Mexico*. Part 1. Washington, DC: Government Printing Office, 1911.

Holm, Tom. "American Indian Warfare: The Cycles of Conflict and the Militarization of Native North America." In *A Companion to American Indian History*, edited by Philip J. Deloria and Neal Salisbury, 154–72. Malden, MA: Blackwell, 2004.

Horn, James, ed. *Captain John Smith: Writings with other Narratives of Roanoke, Jamestown, and the First English Settlement of America*. New York: Library of America, 2007.

Horwitz, Henry. *Parliament, Policy and Politics in the Reign of William III*. Manchester, UK: Manchester University Press, 1977.

Hudson, Angela Pulley. *Creek Paths and Federal Roads: Indians, Settlers, and Slaves in the Making of the American South*. Chapel Hill: University of North Carolina Press, 2010.

Hudson, Charles. *The Juan Pardo Expeditions: Explorations of the Carolinas and Tennessee, 1566–1568*. Rev. ed. Tuscaloosa: University Press of Alabama, 2005.

———. *Knights of Spain, Warriors of the Sun: Hernando de Soto and the South's Ancient Chiefdoms*. Athens: University of Georgia Press, 1997.

———. *The Southeastern Indians*. Knoxville: University of Tennessee Press, 1976.

Hudson, Charles, and Carmen Chaves Tesser, eds. *The Forgotten Centuries: Indians and Europeans in the American South, 1521–1704*. Athens: University of Georgia Press, 1994.

Hulme, Peter, and Tim Youngs, eds. *The Cambridge Companion to Travel Writing*. Cambridge: Cambridge University Press, 2002.

Hume, Robert D. "The Economics of Culture in London, 1660–1740." *Huntington Library Quarterly* 69, no. 4 (2006): 487–533.

Iannini, Christopher P. *Fatal Revolutions: Natural History, West Indian Slavery, and the Routes of American Literature*. Chapel Hill: Omohundro Institute of Early American History and Culture / University of North Carolina Press, 2012.

Inabinet, Joan A., and L. Glen Inabinet. *A History of Kershaw County, South Carolina*. Columbia: University of South Carolina Press, 2011.

"Indians of Southern Virginia, 1650–1711: Depositions in the Virginia and North Carolina Boundary Case." *Virginia Magazine of History and Biography* 7, no. 4 (1900): 337–58.

Isenberger, Dennis. *Native Americans in Early North Carolina: A Documentary History*. Chapel Hill: University of North Carolina Press, 2013.

Ivers, Larry E. *This Torrent of Indians: War on the Southern Frontier, 1715–1728*. Columbia: University of South Carolina Press, 2016.

Johnson, Michael F. "Cactus Hill Archaeology Site." *Encyclopedia Virginia*. Virginia Humanities, 2016. http://www.EncyclopediaVirginia.org/Cactus_Hill_Archaeology_Site.

Journal of the House of Lords. Vol. 16, 1696–1701. London: His Majesty's Stationery Office, 1767–1830. 713–15. British History Online. http://www.british-history.ac.uk/lords-jrnl/vol16/pp713-715.

Keel, Bennie C., and Joffre L. Coe. "A Reconnaissance and Proposal for Archeological Salvage in Falls Reservoir, N.C." (1970). Environmental Statement (rev.). Appendix 5. Wilmington, NC: US Army Corps of Engineers, 1973.

Kelton, Paul. *Cherokee Medicine, Colonial Germs: An Indigenous Nation's Fight against Smallpox, 1518–1824*. Norman: University of Oklahoma Press, 2015.

———. *Epidemics and Enslavement: Biological Catastrophe in the Native Southeast, 1492–1715*. Lincoln: University of Nebraska Press, 2007.

———. "Great Southeastern Smallpox Epidemic, 1696–1700: The Region's First Major Epidemic." In *Transformation of the Southeastern Indians, 1540–1760*, edited by Robbie Ethridge and Charles Hudson, 21–37. Jackson: University Press of Mississippi, 2002.

Kupperman, Karen Ordahl, ed. *Captain John Smith: A Select Edition of His Writings*. Chapel Hill: Omohundro Institute of Early American History and Culture / University of North Carolina Press, 1988.

———. *Indians and English: Facing Off in Early America*. Ithaca, NY: Cornell University Press, 2000.

———. "Perceptions of Treachery, 1583–1640: The Case of the American 'Savages.'" *Historical Journal* 20, no. 2 (1977): 263–87.

Laslett, Peter. *The World We Have Lost: England before the Industrial Age*. 3rd ed. New York: Charles Scribner's Sons, 1984.

Lassiter, Luke E. "Authoritative Texts, Collaborative Ethnography, and Native American Studies." *American Indian Quarterly* 24, no. 4 (2000): 601–14.

La Vere, David. *The Tuscarora War: Indians, Settlers, and the Fight for the Carolina Colonies*. Chapel Hill: University of North Carolina Press, 2013.

Lawson, John. *A New Voyage to Carolina.* [1709]. Edited by Hugh Talmage Lefler. Chapel Hill: University of North Carolina Press, 1967.

Lederer, John. *The Discoveries of John Lederer.* In *The First Explorations of the Trans-Allegheny Region by Virginians, 1650–1674,* edited by Charles Walworth Alvord and Lee Bidgood, 131–71. Cleveland: Arthur H. Clark, 1912.

Lefler, Hugh Talmage. Introduction to *A New Voyage to Carolina,* by John Lawson. Edited by Hugh Talmage Lefler, xi–liv. Chapel Hill: University of North Carolina Press, 1967.

LeMaster, Michelle. "War, Masculinity, and Alliances on the Carolina Frontiers." In *Creating and Contesting Carolina: Proprietary Era Histories,* edited by Michelle LeMaster and Bradford J. Wood, 164–85. Columbia: University of South Carolina Press, 2013.

LeMaster, Michelle, and Bradford J. Wood, eds. *Creating and Contesting Carolina: Proprietary Era Histories.* Columbia: University of South Carolina Press, 2013.

Levander, Carolina F., and Robert S. Levine, eds. *Hemispheric American Studies.* New Brunswick, NJ: Rutgers University Press, 2008.

Lewis, G. Malcolm, ed. *Cartographic Encounters: Perspectives on Native American Mapmaking and Map Use.* Chicago: University of Chicago Press, 1998.

Lockridge, Kenneth A. *The Diary, and Life, of William Byrd II of Virginia, 1674–1744.* Chapel Hill: Omohundro Institute of Early American History and Culture / University of North Carolina Press, 1987.

Loughton, Edward, and Richard Tranter. Memorial [to the Board of Trade]. 26 July 1700. CO 5/1260/f. 234–234v. National Archives, Kew, Surrey, UK.

Maccubbin, Robert P., and Martha Hamilton-Phillips, eds. *The Age of William III and Mary II: Power, Politics, and Patronage, 1688–1702.* Williamsburg, VA: College of William and Mary Press, 1989.

Mancall, Peter C., ed. *The Atlantic World and Virginia, 1550–1624.* Chapel Hill: Omohundro Institute of Early American History and Culture / University of North Carolina Press, 2007.

Mancall, Peter C., and James H. Merrell, eds. *American Encounters: Natives and Newcomers from European Contact to Indian Removal, 1500–1850.* 2nd ed. New York: Routledge, 2007.

Mansell, Ken. *Christ's Hospital Pupils, 1552–1902.* Twickenham, UK: Ashwater Press, 2014.

Mathers, Clay, Jeffrey M. Mitchem, and Charles M. Haecker, eds. *Native and Spanish New Worlds: Sixteenth-Century Entradas in the American Southwest and Southeast.* Tucson: University of Arizona Press, 2013.

McAvoy, Joseph M. "Analysis of Woodland and Historic Period Occupation at the Cactus Hill Site." In *Archaeological Investigations of Site 44SX202, Cactus Hill, Sussex County, Virginia,* edited by Joseph M. McAvoy and Lynn D. McAvoy. Richmond: Virginia Department of Historic Resources, 1997.

McAvoy, Joseph M., and Lynn D. McAvoy. *Archaeological Investigations of Site 44SX202,*

Cactus Hill, Sussex County, Virginia. Richmond: Virginia Department of Historic Resources, 1997.

McCord, David J., ed. *The Statutes at Large of South Carolina.* Vol. 7, *Containing the Acts Relating to Charleston, Courts, Slaves, and Rivers.* Columbia, SC: A. S. Johnston, 1840.

McIlwaine, Henry R., ed. *Journals of the House of Burgesses of Virginia, 1695–1696, 1696–1697, 1698, 1699, 1700–1702.* Richmond, 1913.

Merrell, James H. "Coming to Terms with Early America." *William and Mary Quarterly* 69, no. 3 (July 2012): 535–40.

———. *The Indians' New World: Catawbas and Their Neighbors from European Contact through the Era of Removal.* Chapel Hill: University of North Carolina Press, 2009.

———. "Our Bond of Peace: Patterns of Intercultural Exchange in the Carolina Piedmont, 1650–1750." In *Powhatan's Mantle: Indians in the Colonial Southeast,* edited by Gregory A. Waselkov, Peter H. Wood, and M. Thomas Hatley, 267–304. Lincoln: University of Nebraska Press, 2006.

———. "Second Thoughts on Colonial Historians and American Indians." *William and Mary Quarterly* 69, no. 3 (July 2012): 451–512.

———. "Some Thoughts on Colonial Historians and American Indians." *William and Mary Quarterly* 46, no. 1 (Jan. 1989): 94–119.

———. "Their Very Bones Shall Fight: The Catawba-Iroquois Wars." In *Beyond the Covenant Chain: The Iroquois and Their Neighbors in Indian North America, 1600–1800,* edited by Daniel K. Richter and James H. Merrell, 115–33. University Park: Pennsylvania State University Press, 2003.

———. "'This Western World': The Evolution of the Piedmont, 1525–1725." In *The Siouan Project: Seasons 1 and II,* edited by Roy S. Dickens, H. Trawick Ward Jr., and R. P. Stephen Davis Jr., 19–27. Chapel Hill: University of North Carolina, 1987.

Merrens, H. Roy, ed. *The Colonial South Carolina Scene: Contemporary Views, 1697–1774.* Columbia: University of South Carolina Press, 1977.

Milanich, Jerald, and Charles Hudson. *Hernando de Soto and the Indians of Florida.* Gainesville: University Press of Florida, 1993.

Miller, Jay. *Ancestral Mounds: Vitality and Volatility of Native America.* Lincoln: University of Nebraska Press, 2015.

Montagu, Charles. "A catalogue of the entire and valuable collection of paintings, bronzes, busts in porphyry and marble, and other curiosities, of the most noble Charles Earl of Halifax, deceased. Which will be sold by auction, on Thursday the 6th of March next [1739/40]." British Library, London.

———. Portrait of Charles Montagu, after Michael Dahl. 1985.34. Virginia Museum of History and Culture, Richmond.

———. "To be sold by auction . . . a collection of manuscripts . . . relating to the manufactures, commerce . . . of England, in the reigns of King William and Queen Anne. Collected by the . . . Earl of Halifax, etc." 1760. British Library, London.

Mooney, James. *The Siouan Tribes of the East.* Washington, DC: Government Printing Office, 1894.

Moore, James. Letter to Edward Randolph. 1 March 1699. CO 5/1258/ff. 75–76. National Archives, Kew, Surrey, UK.

———. Letter to [Thomas] Cutler. 3 April 1699. CO 5/1258/ff. 82–83. National Archives, Kew, Surrey, UK.

———. Letter to Thomas Cutler. 25 December 1700. CO 5/1260/f.331–331v. National Archives, Kew, Surrey, UK.

Morris, Michael P. *The Bringing of Wonder: Trade and the Indians of the Southeast, 1700–1783.* Westport, CT: Greenwood Press, 1999.

Moseley, Edward. *A New and Correct Map of the Province of North Carolina.* London, 1733.

Mt. Pleasant, Alyssa, Caroline Wigginton, and Kelly Wisecup. "Materials and Methods in Native American and Indigenous Studies." *Early American Literature* 53, no. 2 (2018): 407–44.

Myer, William Edward. "Indian Trails of the Southeast." In *Forty-Second Annual Report of the Bureau of American Ethnology, 1924–1925,* 727–857. Washington, DC: Government Printing Office, 1928.

Nabokov, Peter. "Orientations from Their Side: Dimensions of Native American Cartographic Discourse." In *Cartographic Encounters: Perspectives on Native American Mapmaking and Map Use,* edited by Lewis G. Malcolm, 241–69. Chicago: University of Chicago Press, 1998.

Navin, John J. *The Grim Years: Settling South Carolina, 1670–1720.* Columbia: University of South Carolina Press, 2020.

Needham, James, and Gabriel Arthur. "The Journeys of Needham and Arthur." In *The First Explorations of the Trans-Allegheny Region by the Virginians, 1650–1674,* edited by Charles Walworth Alvord and Lee Bidgood, 207–27. Cleveland: Arthur H. Clark, 1912.

———. "The Travels of James Needman and Gabriel Arthur through Virginia, North Carolina, and Beyond, 1673–1674." Edited by R. P. Stephen Davis Jr. *Southern Indian Studies* 39 (1990): 31–55.

Norris, Allen Wilkinson Hart. *Beaufort County, North Carolina Deed Book I, 1696–1729: Records of Bath County, North Carolina.* Washington, DC: Beaufort County Historical Society, 2003.

Nutting, P. Bradley. "The Madagascar Connection: Parliament and Piracy, 1690–1701." *American Journal of Legal History* 22, no. 3 (1978): 202–15.

Oatis, Steven J. *A Colonial Complex: South Carolina's Frontiers in the Era of the Yamasee War, 1680–1730.* Lincoln: University of Nebraska Press, 2004.

Oberg, Michael. *Dominion and Civility: English Imperialism and Native America, 1585–1685.* Ithaca, NY: Cornell University Press, 2004.

———. *The Head in Edward Nugent's Hand: Roanoke's Forgotten Indians.* Philadelphia: University of Pennsylvania Press, 2008.

Oberg, Michael, and David Moore. "Voyages to Carolina: Europeans in the Indians' Old World." In *New Voyages to Carolina: Reinterpreting North Carolina History,* edited by Larry E. Tise and Jeffrey J. Crow, 41–59. Chapel Hill: University of North Carolina Press, 2017.

Onnekink, David. "Anglo-French Negotiations on the Spanish Partition Treaties (1698–1700): A Re-evaluation." In *The Contending Kingdoms: France and England 1420–1700,* edited by Glenn Richardson, 161–77. Aldershot, Hants: Ashgate, 2008.

Palmer, William P., ed. *Calendar of Virginia State Papers and Other Manuscripts 1652–1781.* Vol. 1. Richmond, 1875.

Pardee, J. T. and C. F. Park Jr. "Map of the Central Piedmont Region of North Carolina and South Carolina, Showing Location of Mines and Prospects." United States Geological Survey, Professional Paper 213, 1948. In *The Carolina Gold Rush,* by Bruce Roberts. Charlotte, NC: McNally and Loftin, 1972.

Parmenter, Jon. *The Edge of the Woods: Iroquoia, 1534–1701.* East Lansing: Michigan State University Press, 2010.

Parrish, Susan Scott. *American Curiosity: Cultures of Natural History in the Colonial British Atlantic World.* Chapel Hill: Omohundro Institute of Early American History and Culture / University of North Carolina Press, 2006.

Perdue, Theda, and Christopher Arris Oakley. *Native Carolinians: The Indians of North Carolina.* Chapel Hill: University of North Carolina Press, 2010.

Pluckhahn, Thomas J., and Robbie Ethridge, eds. *Light on the Path: The Anthropology and History of the Southeastern Indians.* Tuscaloosa: University of Alabama Press, 2006.

Popple, Henry. *A Map of the British Empire in America.* 1733. London: Willm. Henry Toms and R. W. Seale. F-G 1100 P595. Harry Ransom Center, University of Texas at Austin.

Quinn, David B., ed. *Early Maryland in a Wider World.* Detroit: Wayne State University Press, 1982.

———. *New American World: A Documentary History of America to 1612.* Vol. 5, *The Extension of Settlement in Florida, Virginia, and the Spanish Southwest.* New York: Arno Press, 1979.

Ramsey, William L. *The Yamasee War: A Study of Culture, Economy, and Conflict in the Colonial South.* Lincoln: University of Nebraska Press, 2008.

Randolph, Edward. Letter to [Thomas Egerton, Earl of] Bridgewater. 22 March 1699. CO 5/1258/ff. 77–79. National Archives, Kew, Surrey, UK.

Rhoades, Matthew L. *Long Knives and the Longhouse: Anglo-Iroquois Politics and the Expansion of Colonial Virginia.* Madison, NJ: Fairleigh Dickinson University Press, 2011.

Rice, James D. "Bacon's Rebellion in Indian Country." *Journal of American History* 101, no. 3 (Dec. 2014): 726–50.

———. *Tales from a Revolution: Bacon's Rebellion and the Transformation of Early America.* New York: Oxford University Press, 2012.

Richardson, Glenn, ed. *The Contending Kingdoms: France and England 1420–1700.* Aldershot, Hants: Ashgate, 2008.

Richter, Daniel K. *Before the Revolution: America's Ancient Pasts.* Cambridge, MA: Harvard University Press, 2011.

———. *Facing East from Indian Country: A Native History of Early America.* Cambridge, MA: Harvard University Press, 2001.

———. "Ordeals of the Longhouse: The Five Nations in Early American History." In *Beyond the Covenant Chain: The Iroquois and Their Neighbors in Indian North America, 1600–1800,* edited by Daniel K. Richter and James H. Merrell, 11–27. University Park: Pennsylvania State University Press, 2003.

———. *The Ordeal of the Longhouse: The Peoples of the Iroquois League in the Era of European Colonization.* Chapel Hill: Omohundro Institute of Early American History and Culture / University of North Carolina Press, 2011.

———. *Trade, Land, Power: The Struggle for Eastern North America.* Philadelphia: University of Pennsylvania Press, 2013.

Richter, Daniel K., and James H. Merrell, eds. *Beyond the Covenant Chain: The Iroquois and Their Neighbors in Indian North America, 1600–1800.* University Park: Pennsylvania State University Press, 2003.

Rights, Douglas L. *The American Indian in North Carolina.* Winston-Salem, NC: John F. Blair / Wachovia Historical Society, 1995.

———. "The Trading Path to the Indians." *North Carolina Historical Review* 8, no. 4 (Oct. 1931): 403–26.

Rindfleisch, Bryan C. *Brothers of Coweta: Kinship, Empire, and Revolution in the Eighteenth-Century Muscogee World.* Columbia: University of South Carolina Press, 2021.

Roberts, Bruce. *The Carolina Gold Rush.* Charlotte, NC: McNally and Loftin, 1972.

Round, Phillip H. "Mississippian Contexts for Early American Studies." *Early American Literature* 53, no. 2 (2018): 445–73.

Rountree, Helen C. *Pocahontas's People: The Powhatan Indians of Virginia through Four Centuries.* Norman: University of Oklahoma Press, 1990.

———. *The Powhatan Indians of Virginia: Their Traditional Culture.* Norman: University of Oklahoma Press, 1989.

———. "Trouble Coming Southward: Emanations through and from Virginia, 1607–1675." In *Transformation of the Southeastern Indians, 1540–1760,* edited by Robbie Ethridge and Charles Hudson, 65–78. Jackson: University Press of Mississippi, 2002.

Rountree, Helen C., and E. Randolph Turner III. *Before and After Jamestown: Virginia's Powhatans and Their Predecessors.* Gainesville: University Press of Florida, 2002.

Rowland, Lawrence Sanders, Alexander Moore, and George C. Rogers Jr., eds. *The History of Beaufort County, South Carolina: 1514–1861.* Columbia: University of South Carolina Press, 1996.

Ruediger, Dylan. "'Neither Utterly to Reject Them, Nor Yet to Drawe Them to Come In': Tributary Subordination and Settler Colonialism in Virginia." *Early American Studies* 18, no. 1 (Winter 2020): 1–31.

Ruymbeke, Bertrand Van. *From New Babylon to Eden: The Huguenots and Their Migration to Colonial South Carolina*. Columbia: University of South Carolina Press, 2006.

Salisbury, Neal. "Indians' Old World: Native Americans and the Coming of the Europeans." In *American Encounters: Natives and Newcomers from European Contact to Indian Removal, 1500–1850*, 2nd ed., edited by Peter C. Mancall and James H. Merrell, 4–24. New York: Routledge, 2007.

Salley, Alexander S., Jr., ed. *Journal of the Commissioners of the Indian Trade of South Carolina, September 20, 1710, to April 12, 1715*. Columbia: Historical Commission of South Carolina, 1926.

———. *Journal of the Commons House of Assembly of South Carolina for the Two Sessions of 1697*. Columbia: Historical Commission of South Carolina, 1913.

———. *Journal of the Commons House of Assembly of South Carolina for the Two Sessions of 1698*. Columbia: Historical Commission of South Carolina, 1914.

———. *Journal of the Commons House of Assembly of South Carolina for the Session Beginning October 30, 1700 and Ending November 16, 1700*. Columbia: Historical Commission of South Carolina, 1924.

———. *Journal of the Commons House of Assembly or South Carolina for 1703*. Columbia: Historical Commission of South Carolina, 1934.

———. *Journal of the Commons House of Assembly of South Carolina, March 6, 1705/6–April 9, 1706*. Columbia: Historical Commission of South Carolina, 1937.

———. *Journal of the Commons House of Assembly of South Carolina, November 20, 1706–February 8, 1706/7*. Columbia: Historical Commission of South Carolina, 1939.

———. "The Maybank Family." *South Carolina Historical and Genealogical Magazine* 40, no. 4 (1939): 115–21.

———. *Narratives of Early Carolina, 1650–1708*. New York: Barnes and Noble, 1953.

Seed, Patricia. *Ceremonies of Possession in Europe's Conquest of the New World, 1492–1640*. New York: Cambridge University Press, 1998.

Shefveland, Kristalyn M. *Anglo-Native Virginia: Trade, Conversion, and Indian Slavery in the Old Dominion, 1646–1722*. Athens: University of Georgia Press, 2016.

Sherman, William H. "Stirrings and Searchings (1500–1700)." In *The Cambridge Companion to Travel Writing*, edited by Peter Hulme and Tim Youngs, 17–36. Cambridge: Cambridge University Press, 2002.

Sirmans, M. Eugene. *Colonial South Carolina: A Political History, 1663–1763*. Chapel Hill: University of North Carolina Press, 1966.

Smith, Henry A. M. "Charleston: The Original Plan and the Earliest Settlers." *South Carolina Historical and Genealogical Magazine* 9, no. 1 (1908): 12–27.

Smith, John [Captain]. *A Generall Historie of Virginia, New-England, and the Summer*

Isles. In *The Literatures of Colonial America: An Anthology,* eds. Susan Castillo and Ivy Schweitzer, 197–203. Malden, MA: Blackwell, 2001.

———. *A Map of Virginia.* In *New American World, A Documentary History of America to 1612.* Vol. 5, *The Extension of Settlement in Florida, Virginia, and the Spanish Southwest,* ed. David B. Quinn, 310–46. New York: Arno Press, 1979.

Smith, John [Speaker]. Letter to the Board of Trade. 1699. CO 5/1259/f. 21. National Archives, Kew, Surrey, UK.

———. Letter to William Popple. 1699. CO 5/1259/f. 387. National Archives, Kew, Surrey, UK.

———. Memorial to the Board of Trade and Plantations. 26 July 1700. CO 5/1260/ff. 232–232v. National Archives, Kew, Surrey, UK.

Smith, John, and Thomas Cutler. Memorial to the Board of Trade. 18 April 1698. T 1/52/ff. 299–300. National Archives, Kew, Surrey, UK.

Smithers, Gregory D. *Native Southerners: Indigenous History from Origins to Removal.* Norman: University of Oklahoma Press, 2019.

Speck, William H. "Religion, Politics, and Society in England." In *The Age of William III and Mary II: Power, Politics, and Patronage, 1688–1702,* edited by Robert P. Maccubbin and Martha Hamilton-Phillips, 49–59. Williamsburg, VA: College of William and Mary Press, 1989.

Sprat, Thomas. *The History of the Royal-Society of London for the Improving of Natural Knowledge.* London, 1667.

Spufford, Margaret. *Small Books and Pleasant Histories: Popular Fiction and Its Readership in Seventeenth-Century England.* New York: Cambridge University Press, 1981.

Stansell, Zoe. Email with the editor. May 31, 2019.

Stanwood, Owen. "Captives and Slaves: Indian Labor, Cultural Conversion, and the Plantation Revolution in Virginia." *Virginia Magazine of History and Biography* 114, no. 4 (2006): 434–63.

———. *The Empire Reformed: English America in the Age of the Glorious Revolution.* Philadelphia: University of Pennsylvania Press, 2011.

Stephenson, Robert L. *A Basic Inventory of Archaeological Sites in South Carolina* [July 1, 1971]. Rev. ed., July 1, 1972. Research Manuscript Series, Book 136. Archaeology and Anthropology, South Carolina Institute of Scholar Commons. http://scholarcommons.sc.edu/archanth_books/136.

Stern, Jessica Yirush. "Economic Philosophies of Indian Trade Regulation Policy in Early South Carolina." In *Creating and Contesting Carolina: Proprietary Era Histories,* edited by Michelle LeMaster and Bradford J. Wood, 97–117. Columbia: University of South Carolina Press, 2013.

———. *The Lives in Objects: Native Americans, British Colonists, and Cultures of Labor and Exchange in the Southeast.* Chapel Hill: University of North Carolina Press, 2017.

Swanton, John R. *The Indians of the Southeastern United States.* Washington, DC: Smithsonian Institution Press, 1979.

BIBLIOGRAPHY

Tanner, Helen Hornbeck. "Land and Water Communication Systems of the Southeastern Indians." In *Powhatan's Mantle: Indians in the Colonial Southeast,* edited by Gregory A. Waselkov, Peter H. Wood, and M. Thomas Hatley, 27–42. Lincoln: University of Nebraska Press, 2006.

Tanner, Henry S. *Map of North and South Carolina.* Philadelphia, 1825.

Tinling, Marion, ed. *The Correspondence of the Three William Byrds of Westover, Virginia, 1684–1776.* 2 vols. Charlottesville: University Press of Virginia, 1977.

Tise, Larry E., and Jeffrey J. Crow, eds. *New Voyages to Carolina: Reinterpreting North Carolina History.* Chapel Hill: University of North Carolina Press, 2017.

Tranter, John. Will of John Tranter. 15 December 1723. MARS Id. 12.96.25.72. State Archives of North Carolina, Raleigh.

Traunter, Richard. "The Travels of Richard Traunter." [ca. 1701]. Mss 5:9 T6945:1. Virginia Museum of History and Culture, Richmond.

———. "The Travels of Richard Traunter." [ca. 1701]. M/583. British Library, London.

Treasury. Representation to King William III. 18 April 1698. T 1/52/ff. 298–99. National Archives, Kew, Surrey, UK.

Treasury. Warrant for John Smith and Thomas Cutler. 30 June 1698. T 60/4/f. 470. National Archives, Kew, Surrey, UK.

Treasury. William III to John Smith and Thomas Cutler. 28 June 1698. T 52/19/f. 515. National Archives, Kew, Surrey, UK.

Trefzer, Annette. *Disturbing Indians: The Archaeology of Southern Fiction.* Tuscaloosa: University of Alabama Press, 2007.

Trigger, Bruce G., and Wilcomb Washburn. *The Cambridge History of the Native Peoples of the Americas.* Vol. 1, *North America.* New York: Cambridge University Press, 1996.

Troxler, Carole W. "Places and People." In *Shuttle and Plow: A History of Alamance County, North Carolina.* Edited by Carole W. Troxler and William M. Vincent, 28–56. Graham, NC: Alamance County Historical Association, 1999.

Tucker, Norma. *Colonial Virginians and Their Maryland Relatives: A Genealogy of the Tucker Family.* Baltimore: Clearfield Publishing, 2002.

US Army Corps of Engineers. Wilmington District and the State of North Carolina. "B. Everett Jordan Dam and Lake Master Plan Update, Draft Report." Wilmington, 2007. ftp://ftp.chathamnc.org/Chatham_ConservationPlan_GIS/Plans_Policies_Ordinances/USACoE_Jordan%20Lake%20Master%20Plan%20Update.pdf.

Vernon, James. Letter to the Lords of the Treasury. 9 May 1698. T 1/52/f. 296. National Archives, Kew, Surrey, UK.

Wachob, Andrew. "Impact of Removing the Granby Dam on Water Levels in the Congaree River." South Carolina Department of Natural Resources: Land, Water and Conservation Division, Water Resources Report 27, 2002. https://dc.statelibrary.sc.gov/bitstream/handle/10827/11269/DNR_Impact_of_Removing_the_Granby_Dam_2002.pdf?sequence=1&isAllowed=y.

BIBLIOGRAPHY

Walsh, Lorena S. *Motives of Honor, Pleasure, and Profit: Plantation Management in the Colonial Chesapeake, 1607-1763*. Chapel Hill: University of North Carolina Press, 2010.

Ward, H. Trawick, and R. P. Stephen Davis Jr. "Introduction to Archaeology of the Historic Occaneechi Indians." *Southern Indian Studies* 36-37 (1988): 1-10.

———. *Time before History: The Archaeology of North Carolina*. Chapel Hill: University of North Carolina Press, 1999.

———. "Tribes and Traders on the North Carolina Piedmont, A.D. 1000-1710." In *Societies in Eclipse: Archaeology of the Eastern Woodlands Indians, A.D. 1400-1700*, edited by David S. Brose, C. Wesley Cowan, and Robert C. Mainfort, 125-41. Tuscaloosa: University of Alabama Press, 2001.

Warren, Stephen. *The Worlds the Shawnees Made: Migration and Violence in Early America*. Chapel Hill: University of North Carolina Press, 2014.

Waselkov, Gregory A. "Exchange and Interaction Since 1500." In *Handbook of North American Indians*, vol. 14, *The Southeast*, edited by Raymond D. Fogelson, 686-96. Washington, DC: Smithsonian Institute, 2004.

———. "Seventeenth-Century Trade in the Colonial Southeast." *Southeastern Archaeology* 8, no. 2 (Winter 1989): 117-33.

Waselkov, Gregory A., and Marvin T. Smith, eds. *Forging Southeastern Identities: Social Archaeology, Ethnohistory, and Folklore of the Mississippian to Early Historic South*. Tuscaloosa: University of Alabama Press, 2017.

Waselkov, Gregory A., Peter H. Wood, and M. Thomas Hatley, eds. *Powhatan's Mantle: Indians in the Colonial Southeast*. Lincoln: University of Nebraska Press, 2006.

Weaver, Jace, Craig S. Womack, and Robert Warrior. *American Literary Nationalism*. Albuquerque: University of New Mexico Press, 2006.

Webber, Mabel L. "The Bond Family of Hobcaw Plantation, Christ Church Parish." *South Carolina Historical and Genealogical Magazine* 25, no. 1 (1924): 1-22.

———. "The First Governor Moore and His Children." *South Carolina Historical and Genealogical Magazine* 37, no. 1 (1936): 1-23.

———. "Hyrne Family." *South Carolina Historical and Genealogical Magazine* 22, no. 4 (1921): 101-18.

———. "Sir Nathaniel Johnson and His Son Robert: Governors of South Carolina." *South Carolina Historical and Genealogical Magazine* 38, no. 4 (1937): 109-15.

Weber, David J. *The Spanish Frontier in North America*. New Haven, CT: Yale University Press, 1992.

Widmer, Randolph J. "The Structure of Southeastern Chiefdoms." In *The Forgotten Centuries: Indians and Europeans in the American South, 1521-1704*, edited by Charles Hudson and Carmen Chaves Tesser, 125-55. Athens: University of Georgia Press, 1994.

Williams, David. *The Georgia Gold Rush: Twenty-Niners, Cherokees, and Gold Fever*. Columbia: University of South Carolina Press, 1993.

Williams, Nancy K., and H. Thomas Foster II. "An Analysis of Native American/Colonialist Interaction in the Southeastern United States." *International Journal of Historical Archeology* 21 (2017): 513–31.

Williamson, Margaret Holmes. *Powhatan Lords of Life and Death: Command and Consent in Seventeenth-Century Virginia.* Lincoln: University of Nebraska Press, 2003.

Wisecup, Kelly. *Medical Encounters: Knowledge and Identity in Early American Literatures.* Amherst: University of Massachusetts Press, 2013.

Withington, Lothrop. "South Carolina Gleanings in England." *South Carolina Historical and Genealogical Magazine* 4, no. 1 (1903): 286–95.

Wood, Peter H. "The Changing Population of the Colonial South: An Overview by Race and Region, 1685–1790." In *Powhatan's Mantle: Indians in the Colonial Southeast,* edited by Gregory A. Waselkov, Peter H. Wood, and M. Thomas Hatley, 57–132. Lincoln: University of Nebraska Press, 2006.

Woodard, Buck, and Danielle Moretti-Langholtz. *The Millie Woodson-Turner Nottoway Reservation Allotment and Farmstead.* College of William and Mary, Department of Anthropology, Archaeological Research Report Series, Number 6 / Commonwealth of Virginia, Department of Historic Resources, Research Report Series, Number 22. 2017.

Wright, J. Leitch, Jr. *The Only Land They Knew: American Indians in the Old South.* Lincoln: University of Nebraska Press, 1999.

Wright, Louis B. "William Byrd I and the Slave Trade." *Huntington Library Quarterly* 8, no. 4 (1945): 379–87.

Index

Acamantiaes Indians: at Ajusher, xxvi, xxvi*n*, 23*n*; in *soc-ca-hick* alliance, xxxv, 23
Adams, Natalie, 30*n*
Adams, Percy G., xxxvi*n*
Ajusheres Indians, xxvi*n*, 23*n*, 38*n*; in *soc-ca-hick* alliance, xxxv, 23; and Tuscaroras, xxxv, 42
Ajusher town: as coalescent community, xxvi, xxvi*n*, xxviii, 23*n*, 38; and Eno Will, xxviii, xxxv, 38; games at, 49*n*; and Lawson, xxvi, 20*n*, 49*n*; location of, xv*n*, xxxi, 35, 38*n*; *soc-ca-hick* ceremony at, xii, xxxv, 39–40, 42; Traunter's route to, xxxi, 38, 43
Albemarle Sound (Ronoque Harbor, Ronoque Sound), xvii*n*, 13, 13*n*, 35, 35*n*
Algonquian Indians: and disease, xxiii; English attack on, xxiii; gifting rituals, xxi, xxii; history in region, xix–xx; Indian–Indian exchange, xxi; and Jamestown colonists, xxiii–xxiv; killing of Wingina, xxiii; kinship alliances, xxi, xxi*n*; political organization, xx, xxii, xxiii, xxiii*n*; and Roanoke colonists, xxii–xxiii; and Spanish, xxii; territory and towns, xx, xxii, xxiii, xxiii*n*, xxiv; trade roads, meaning of, xxi. *See also* Powhatan Indians
alliances, Indigenous: with colonial traders, xxxiv, xxxv*n*; kinship, xxi, xxi*n*, xxii. See also *soc-ca-hick*
Appomattox River (Virginia), xi, xiii, xxx, 3, 11, 12*n*, 36, 36*n*

Appomattox Store: Byrd I's, xv, 9, 11; exchanges with Indians, xviii–xix, xxviii, xxxiii, xxxv*n*; killing of Indians at, xxxiii*n*; location of, 7*n*, 12*n*; Traunter as factor, xi, xv, xix, 9, 63; and Tuscarora Indians, xxxv*n*
Arthur, Gabriel. *See* Needham, James, and Gabriel Arthur
Ashe, Thomas: "Carolina, or a Description of the Present State of that Country," xxxvii
Ayuso, Robert A., 47*n*

Bacon, Nathaniel, xvii, xxv, xxviii, xxxii
Bacon's Rebellion, xxv*n*, xxvii
Barnett, Louise K., xli*n*
Bath, North Carolina (Ronoque town), xvii*n*, 35, 35*n*
Baxter, Stephen B., xiv*n*, xvii*n*
Beck, Robin, xii, xv*n*, xxii*n*, xxiv*n*, xxv, xxvii*n*, 18*n*, 19*n*, 23*n*, 26*n*, 27*n*, 29*n*, 49*n*, 50*n*
Berkhofer, Robert F., Jr., xli*n*
Beverley, Robert, xxxix, 12*n*, 19*n*, 28*n*; *History and Present State of Virginia*, xl
Blake, Gov. Joseph, 58, 58*n*, 67, 67*n*
Bland, Edward, xii*n*, xxxvii, 12*n*; *Discovery of New Brittaine*, xxxvii
Board of Trade (English): and Byrd I, xv; jurisdictional authority, xli; members of, xiii*n*, xviii, 5*n*; and silver project, xiii–xiv, xviii, xxx, xlvi, xlvii, 57–59, 57*n*, 61–64, 62*n*, 65, 67–68
Boudreaux, Edmond, III, xxix, 45*n*

INDEX

Bowne, Eric, xxii*n*, xxiv*n*, xxv*n*
Briceland, Alan V., xv*n*, xvi*n*, xxiv*n*, xxvii*n*, 9*n*, 12*n*, 38*n*, 40*n*
Bridge Creek (South Carolina), 29–30, 29*n*, 52, 52*n*, 53*n*
burial practices: of southeastern Indians, xxv, xxix, 28*n*; of Waxhaw Indians, xxxix, 27–28
Butler, J. Robert, 24*n*
Byrd, Col. William: Appomattox trade store, xi, xv, xviii–xix, xxxiii, xli, 9, 11, 35; and attack on South Carolina traders, xxxiii, xxxiii*n*, 8*n*; and Bacon's Rebellion, xxxii; and Indian Jack, xxxiii, xxxiii*n*, 9; and Indian slave trade, xxiv, xxxii, xxxiii, xxxiv; and Moore, xxxii, xxxiii, xxxvi; and Occaneechis, xxxii; political roles, xv, 9*n*; and Seneca Indians, xxvii*n*; traders (Byrd's), xi, xviii, xxx, xxxiii, xxxiv, xl, xl*n*, xliii, 9, 10, 11, 11*n*, 20, 21, 23, 25, 25*n*; Traunter's employer, xi, xvi, xix, xxxv, 9, 10
Byrd, William, II: on Christianizing Indians, xliii; and Eno Will, xv, xv*n*, xxvi; and Halifax, xvi, xvi*n*; "History of the Dividing Line," xli; on Indian afterlife, 29*n*; "Journey to the Land of Eden," xxvi; on rattlesnakes, xxxix, xxxix*n*; on Seneca warfare, xli; on tigers, 16*n*; on trade girls, xxi*n*; on trade path, 13*n*, 15*n*

Cactus Hill archaeological site, xix, xix*n*, 13*n*
Calcaterra, Angela, xxxviii
Carey, Daniel, xxxviii*n*, xl*n*
Carson, James Taylor, xxi, xxiii*n*
Catawba Indians: in Cofitachequi chiefdom, xx, 49*n*; and Lawson, 18*n*; location of, 9*n*; route from Virginia to, 15*n*; and Seneca Indians, xxvii; stone memorials, 18*n*; and Virginia traders, 7*n*. *See also* Esaw Indians
Catawba path. *See* trade paths/roads
Cherokee Indians: and Long, xxxiv; Tomahittans as, 40*n*; and Virginia traders, 7*n*; and Yuchi Indians, xxxiv, xxxiv*n*
Coe, Joffre L., xxix, 28*n*, 38*n*, 45*n*

Cofitachequi: archaeological evidence of, xxii*n*, 29*n*, 49*n*, 50*n*; location of, xx, xxix; political organization, xx; and Spanish, xxii; and Woodward, xxii
Collet, John, 25*n*, 35*n*, 43*n*, 45*n*
commission, Eno Will's. *See soc-ca-hick*
Commons House of Assembly of South Carolina: and attack on South Carolina traders, 8*n*, 9*n*; and Cutler, xiv*n*; Goose Creek men, xxxiii*n*, 54*n*; and Loughton, xiv*n*; restrictions on Virginia traders, xliii*n*
Congaree Indians: to Charleston, xviii; in Cofitachequi chiefdom, xx, 49*n*; gaming, 49*n*; and Lawson, xliv; location of, 30*n*, 31*n*, 54*n*
Congaree River (South Carolina), xlv, 30, 30*n*, 31*n*, 52, 52*n*, 53*n*, 56*n*, 61*n*
Cooper, Thomas, xlii*n*
Couture, Jean: gold discovery, 66, 67–68; imprisoned in South Carolina, 58, 58*n*, 67–68, 67*n*; and LaSalle, xiv; and silver project, xxx*n*, xlvii, 57, 59
Crane, Verner, xiv*n*
Crittenden, Charles C., 43*n*, 44*n*
Cutler, Thomas: London gentleman, xiv, xvii*n*; and Moore, 59*n*, 62*n*; related to Loughton and Maybank, xiv*n*; silver project partner, xiv, 65, 65*n*; and Smith, xiv, 62*n*; in South Carolina, xiv*n*

Dahlberg, Sandra L., xxxi*n*, 47*n*, 59*n*
Daniel, I. Randolph, Jr., 24*n*
Davis, R. P. Stephen, Jr., xxvii, xxxiv*n*, xxxvii*n*, 15*n*, 18*n*, 19*n*, 23*n*, 37*n*, 40*n*
Deep River (North Carolina), 22, 22*n*, 23, 43–44, 43*n*
De Krey, Gary Stuart, xiv*n*
Dickens, Roy S., 19*n*
diplomatic protocols, English, 19–20, 19*n*
diplomatic protocols, Indigenous: alliances, xxviii, xxxi*n*, xxxv, 21, 23, 39–40, 42; food gifts to visitors, xxii, xliv, 20, 21, 27, 39; gifting, xxi, xxii, xlii, 20, 21, 39, 50, 59, 64; greeting visitors, xxi, xxii–xxiii, 19–20, 20*n*; refusals of hospitality to colonists, xxiii, xlii, xliv, 49. *See also soc-ca-hick*

INDEX

disease: among southeastern Indians, xii, xxiii, xxv–xxvi, 26*n*; at Suteree town, xliv, 26; at Waxhaw town, xxxix, 27. *See also* smallpox

doctors, Indigenous: healing practices, xii, 26, 26*n*, 27. *See also* burial practices; healing practices

Dudley, Paul, xxxix*n*

Dunbar-Ortiz, Roxanne, xxvii*n*, xliv*n*

Edgar, Walter, xv*n*, 58*n*

Eno Fields: as abandoned Eno town, xii, xxvi, 18; archaeological remains near, 18*n*; description of, 18, 37*n*; and Shakori Indians, xxvi, 18; stone memorials near, xxviii, 18; Tuscarora attack on, xxvi, 18, 37*n*

Eno Indians: at Ajusher, xxvi, xxvi*n*, 23*n*; and Shakori Indians, xxvi; in *soc-ca-hick* alliance, xxxv, 23; and Tuscarora Indians, xxvi, xxxv, 18; at Waxhaw village, 49

Eno River (North Carolina), xxvi, 8*n*, 18*n*, 19*n*

Eno Will: Ajusher's headman, xii, xxvi, 38; as allied with English, 20, 38, 39; and Byrd II, xv, xv*n*, xxvi; at Keyauwee Town, xxviii, 23; and Lawson, xv, xv*n*, xxvi, xxviii, 20*n*; narrator of Occaneechi-Tomahittan story, 40–42; and Occaneechis, xxvii, xl*n*, 20, 20*n*, 23, 38, 40, 42; physical description of, xxviii, 39; political influence, xxviii, 49; as Shacco-Will, xv*n*; and *soc-ca-hick*, xii, xxxi*n*, xxxiv, xxxv, xxxv*n*, 21, 22, 23, 24, 38, 39, 40, 42, 49; traveled with Traunter, xv, xxx, xxxi, xxxi*n*, xlii, 22–24, 35, 42, 43–50; and Tuscarora Indians, xxviii, 42; at Waxhaw village, xxviii, xlii, xliv, 49, 50; and Will's servant, xxxi, xxxi*n*, 22, 43, 44, 45, 46, 49, 50

Esaw Indians: and Byrd's traders, xxx, 9, 25*n*; in Cofitachequi chiefdom, xx, 49*n*; and South Carolina, xviii, 9*n*. *See also* Catawba Indians

Ethridge, Robbie, xx*n*, xxi*n*, xxvi*n*, xxxiii, 15*n*, 23*n*

European goods: for exchanges, 59, 64; given at Occaneechi Town, xlii, 20; given at Waxhaw village, 50

Everett, C. S., xxxvi

Fecher, Rebecca, 22*n*, 25*n*

Feeley, Stephen, xxxii, xxxvi

Field, Ophelia, xlvi*n*

Fitts, Mary E., xxi*n*, 26*n*

Five Nations. *See* Iroquois Indians

Floyd, Viola C., 29*n*

Foley, Nora K., 47*n*

Fort Henrico/Fort Henry, xii*n*, xxiv

Fothergill, Augusta B., xxx*n*

Fry, Joshua, xxvi*n*, 11*n*, 13*n*, 23*n*

Gallay, Alan, xxxii, xxxii*n*, xxxiii*n*, 10*n*

games: at Ajusher, 49*n*; by Congarees, 49*n*; at Waxhaw village, 49

Gascoigne, John, xxxvii*n*, xxxviii*n*

Geniton-Tar River (North Carolina), xxvi, xxvi*n*, 18, 18*n*, 37, 37*n*, 38

Good, William: death of, xiv*n*, 61, 65, 67; employed by Pembroke, xiv, 61*n*; silver project partner, xiv, 61, 65, 67, 68

Goose Creek (South Carolina), 32*n*, 55, 55*n*

Goose Creek men: and Moore, xv, xxxiii*n*, 8*n*, 54*n*; political faction, xv, xxxiii*n*, 54*n*

Granganimeo, xxii. *See also* Algonquian Indians

Great Alamance Creek (North Carolina), xxvi*n*, 23*n*

Halifax, 1st Earl of (Charles Montagu): and Board of Trade, xiii*n*, xviii, xli, 5*n*; Byrd II, xvi, xvi*n*; dedicatee of *Travels*, xlvi, 5; literary patron, xlvi–xlvii, xlvii*n*; and silver project, xiii*n*, xviii, xli, xli*n*, xlvi, 5*n*, 62*n*; and Smith, xiv*n*, xvii

Hall, Joseph M., xix*n*

Hammett, Julia E., 18*n*

Hanna, Mark G., xxviii*n*, 23–24*n*

Hatcher's Run (North Carolina), 17, 17*n*, 37, 37*n*

Haw River, xxviii, 22, 22*n*, 43, 43*n*

healing practices: at Suteree Town, xii, 26, 26*n*; at Waxhaw Town, xii, 27

89

Hearn (Herne), John: attack on, xxxiii, 8–9, 8*n*, 40–42; death, xv*n*; as Moore's trader, xxxiii, 8; as South Carolina slave trader, xxxiii–xxxiv; as South Carolina trader, xxxiii, xxxiii*n*, 8, 31*n*
Herbert, Thomas. *See* Pembroke, 8th Earl of
Hodge, Frederick Webb, 16*n*
Holm, Tom, xxv*n*
Horwitz, Henry, xiv*n*
House of Burgesses (Virginia): and attack on South Carolina traders, xxxiii*n*, 8*n*; and Byrd I, xv, xxxiii*n*, 8*n*, 9*n*
House of Lords (English): and Edward Tranter, xviii, xviii*n*; *Journal of the House of Lords*, xviii*n*
Howes, Job, xv, 54, 54*n*
Hudson, Charles, xx*n*, xxii*n*, xxv*n*, xxvi*n*, 23*n*
Hume, Robert, xvii*n*

Iannini, Christopher, xxxviii
Inabinet, Joan A., 29*n*
Inabinet, L. Glen, 29*n*
Indian Jack: at Appomattox store with Traunter, 9; attack on, xxxiii, 8–9, 40–42; enslaved by Moore, xv, xxx, xxxiii, 8, 8*n*, 19; at Occaneechi Town, xxxiv, 19–20; as slave raider, xxxiii–xxxiv, 9–10; traveled with Traunter, xv, xxx, 11*n*; as Wateree, xv*n*, xxxiii, 9; as Wateree Jack, xv, xv*n*, 8*n*; on Waxhaw afterlife, 28, 28*n*
Indian slave trade: and Bacon's Rebellion, xxv*n*; and Byrd I, xxiv, xxxii, xxxiii, xxxiv; Indian middlemen, xxv, xxxii; intercolonial competition for, xxxii, xxxiii, xlii*n*; and Moore, xv, xxxii, xxxiv, 8*n*; and Occaneechis, xxv, xxxii, xxxiii–xxxiv, xxxv, xl, 9–10, 10*n*; and Saxapahaws, xxxiii–xxxiv, 9–10, 10*n*; and smallpox, xii, xxv, xxvi; and South Carolina, xxv, xxix, xxxii–xxxiii, xxxiii*n*, xxxiv, xxxvi, xl, 8*n*, 10*n*; and Spanish, xxii; and Traunter, xxxiii, xxxiv; and Tuscaroras, xxix; and Virginia, xxiv, xxv, xxv*n*, xxxii, xxxiii, xxxiii*n*, xxxiv, 10*n*; and Waterees, xxxii, xxxiii, xxxvi, 9–10, 10*n*; and Westos, xxiv, xxv, xxxii
"Indians of Southern Virginia, 1650–1711," 13*n*
Iroquois Indians: captives of mourning wars, xxiv–xxv; Haudenosaunee (Five Nations), xxvi, xxviii; locations of, xxiv, xxvi, 18*n*; mourning wars, xxiv. *See also* Seneca Indians; Seneca-Siouan hostilities; Tuscarora Indians; Westo Indians
Ivers, Larry E., xv*n*, xxxiii*n*, 8*n*, 31*n*

Jefferson, Peter, xxvi*n*, 11*n*, 13*n*, 23*n*
Johnson, Michael F., xix*n*
Johnson, Nathaniel, xv, 54, 54*n*
Jones, Cadwallader, xxiv, xxvii

Keel, Bennie C., 38*n*
Kelton, Paul, xii, xxi*n*, 26*n*
Keyauwee Indians: archaeological evidence, 23*n*; Keyauwee Town, xi, 24; location of, xv*n*, xxviii; "new" path near, xxxi, xxxi*n*; and Saxapahaws, 23; in *soc-ca-hick* alliance, xxviii, xxxi*n*, 22, 23; as suspects in attack on South Carolina traders, xxxiii, 8*n*
Knap of Reeds Creek (North Carolina), 17, 17*n*, 37, 37*n*

Laslett, Peter, xvi*n*
La Vere, David, xviii*n*, xxi*n*, xxvi, xxix*n*, xxxii, xxxiii, 18*n*, 19*n*
Lawson, John: and Ajusher, 38*n*; on Christianizing Indians, xliii; and Eno Will, xv, xv*n*, xxvi, xxviii, 20*n*; on Indian afterlife, 28*n*; on Indian food, xliv, xlv, 12*n*; on Indian slaves, xxv; on Indigenous games, 49*n*; *New Voyage to Carolina*, xviii, xlii; route from Charleston, 7*n*, 11, 11*n*; on Seneca Indians, xxvi*n*; on smallpox, 26*n*; on stone memorials, xxvii, 18*n*; on trade girls, xxi*n*; and Tuscarora Indians, xviii
Lederer, John: *Discoveries of John Lederer*, xxxvii; excursion of 1670, xxxix; gunfire greeting, 19*n*; on rattlesnakes, xxxix; on stone memorials, 18*n*

INDEX

Lefler, Hugh Talmage, xliin, 30n, 31n, 54n

Legaré, Solomon: as Charleston silversmith, xxx, xxxn, xliv, 64n; Frenchman with Traunter, xxxn, xliv–xlv, 11n, 36n, 45; and silver project, xxx, xxxn, 11n, 59, 64n, 68

LeMaster, Michelle, xxxvn

Long, Alexander, xxxiv, xxxv

Lords Proprietor of Carolina, xxxii, xxxviin, 63n

Loughton, Edward: "Humble Memorial of Edward Loughton and Richard Tranter," xlvii, 57–59, 57n; occupations, xiv, xivn; political roles in Charleston, xivn; related to Cutler and Maybank, xivn; silver project partner, xiii, xxx, xxxn, xxxin, 57–59, 62, 63, 64, 66, 67, 67n, 68; traveled with Traunter, xxx, 11n

Mansell, Ken, xvin

Maybank, David: in Charleston, xiv, xivn, xxxin; related to Cutler and Loughton, xivn; silver project partner, xiv, xxx, xxxn, 59, 67, 67n, 68; traveled with Traunter, xxx, 11n

McAvoy, James P., xixn, 13n

McAvoy, Joseph, xixn

McAvoy, Lynn D., xixn

McCord, David J., xivn

McIlwaine, Henry R., xxxiiin, 8n

Meherrin Indians: location of, 40, 40n; town, xiin

Meherrin River (Virginia), 15, 37, 37n

Mellon, Paul, xiiin, xlvii, xlviii, 65n

memorials, Indian: of stones, xxvii, 18, 18n

Merrell, James H., xvn, xvin, xviiin, xixn, xxi, xxiiin, xxv, xxvn, xxviin, xxviii, xxxiiin, xxxivn, xxxvn, xxxvin, xliiin, 9n, 18n

Mitchem, Jeffrey M., xxn

Monacan Indians, xxiii, 18n; town, xxiv

Moniseep Ford, xii, 15n, 37n

Monks Neck oldfields: description of, 12; as Manks Nessoneicks oldfield, xiin, 12n

Montagu, Charles. See Halifax, 1st Earl of

Moore, David, xxiin, xxiiin

Moore, Gov. James: and Byrd I, xxxii, xxxiii, xxxvi, 8; employer of Hearn and Stevens, xxxiii, 8; and Goose Creek men, xv, xxxiiin; Indian Jack's enslaver, xv, xxx, xxxiii; and Indian slave trade, xv, xvn, xxxii, xxxiii, xxxiv, 8n; interference with silver project, xiii, 58n, 59n, 62, 62n, 63, 65, 66; silver discovery, 65, 65n; and Traunter, xlv, 32, 34, 54, 55

Morris, Michael P., xvin, xxvn

Moseley, Edward, xvii, xviin

mourning wars, captives of, xxiv. See also Indian slave trade; slaves, Indian

Myer, William E., 17n

natural history, xxvi, xxxvii, xxxviii, xl

Navin, John J., 63n

Needham, James, and Gabriel Arthur: narrative, xxxvii, xxxviin, xl, xln; and Tomahittan Indians, xxxivn, 40n

Netherton, Henry: and silver project, xxx, xxxn, 11n, 59, 59n; traveled with Traunter, xxx, xxxi, 11n, 36n; as Virginia planter-surveyor, xxx, xxxn

Nicholson, Gov. Francis: and Indian policy, xxxv, xxxvn

Norris, Allen W. H., xviin

Nottoway Indians: complaint against Tuscaroras, xxxvn; and Nicholson, xxxvn; towns, xiin

Nottoway River (Virginia), xix, xxxin, 8, 13, 36–37

Nutting, Bradley, 23–24n

Oatis, Steven J., xvn, xxn, xxxivn, xliii, 8n

Oberg, Michael, xxin, xxiin, xxiiin, xxviii, 39n

Occaneechi Indians: and Bacon's Rebellion, xxv, xxvn; and Byrd I, xxxiv; and Byrd's traders, xln, 20, 21; as captives, xxxiv, 9–10; and Eno Will, xvn, xxxv, xxxvi, 20–21, 20n, 38–40; food gifts to Traunter, xliv, 20; and Indian Jack, xxxiv, 19–20, 21; middlemen in Indian slave trade, xxv, xxxii; and Seneca-Siouan hostilities, xxvii, xxviii; as slave raiders, xxv; in soc-ca-hick alliance,

91

Occaneechi Indians (*continued*)
xxvii, xxxi*n*, xxxv, 21, 23, 38, 40; *soc-ca-hick* as anti-Occaneechi pact, xxxv; and South Carolina slave raiders, xxix, xxxiv, 8; as threat to trade, 8, 38–39; and Traunter, 19–21; and Wateree slave raiders, xxxiii–xxxiv, 9–10, 10*n*; women, xlii, xliv, 20

Occaneechi-Tomahittan attack, xxxiv, xxxiv*n*, xl, xliii, 8, 41–42

Occaneechi Town: and Ajusher, 38*n*; archaeological evidence of, xxxv–xxxvi*n*, 19*n*, 28*n*; location of, xxvii, 8*n*, 15*n*; "new" road near, xxxi; population of, in 1698, xxxv, xxxv*n*; and Traunter, xi, xxxiv, xlii, xliv

Onnekink, David, xlvi*n*

Palmer, William P., xxviii*n*, xxxiii*n*, xxxv*n*

Pamlico River (North Carolina), xvii, xvii*n*, xviii, xx

Pardee, J. T., xxxi*n*, 47*n*

Park, C. F., Jr., xxxi*n*, 47*n*

Parrish, Susan Scott, xxxvii*n*, xxxviii, xl*n*

peacemaking. *See soc-ca-hick*

Pembroke, 8th Earl of (Thomas Herbert), xiii*n*, xiv, xviii, 61*n*, 62, 62*n*

Popple, Henry, xxvi*n*, 23*n*

Powhatan Indians: and English colonists, xxiii, xxiv; political organization and leaders, xx, xx*n*, xxii, xxiii, xxiii*n*, xxiv; and Siouan groups, xxiii; territory, xxii, xxiv; towns, xx, xxiii, xxiv

Ramsey, William L., xxxii*n*

Randolph, Edward, xiv*n*, 61*n*, 62*n*, 65*n*

religion: Indian afterlife, 28*n*; Waxhaw afterlife, xxxix, xliii, 28

Rhoades, Matthew L., xxvii*n*

Rice, James D., xvii*n*, xxv*n*, xxxii*n*; xxxv

Richter, Daniel K., xxiv, xxv, xl, xli, xli*n*, xxxv*n*

Rights, Douglas, 22*n*, 25*n*, 38*n*

rituals, Indigenous: burial, xxv, xxix, 27–28; greeting, 19–20, 20*n*; healing, 26, 26*n*, 27; mourning, 27

Roanoke colony, xxii–xxiii, xxiii*n*

Roanoke Island, xx, xxii, xxiii, xxiii*n*

Roanoke River, xii, xii*n*, xxviii, 8, 15–16, 15*n*, 18*n*, 37, 37*n*

Roberts, Bruce, xxxi*n*

Ronoque Harbor, Ronoque Sound. *See* Albemarle Sound

Ronoque town. *See* Bath, North Carolina

Round, Phillip, xx–xxi, xxx*n*

Rountree, Helen C., xx*n*, xxiii*n*, xxiv*n*, xliii*n*

Royal Society of London, xvi*n*, xxxvii, xxxvii*n*, xxxviii, xxxviii*n*, xxxix*n*, xl, xlv

Ruymbeke, Bertrand Van, xxx*n*

Salisbury, Neal, xxi*n*

Salley, Alexander S., Jr., xiv*n*, xxxiii*n*, xxxvii*n*, 8*n*, 9*n*, 54*n*, 58*n*, 67*n*

Santee Indians, xx, 26*n*, 31*n*, 49*n*; Santee town, xi, 26*n*

Santee River (South Carolina), xxxiii*n*, xlv, 26*n*, 30*n*, 31–32, 31*n*, 53, 53*n*, 54, 54*n*, 61*n*

Saponi Indians: at Ajusher, xxvi, xxvi*n*, 23*n*; in *soc-ca-hick* alliance, xxxv, 23

Savana Hutts, xlv, 30*n*, 53, 53–54*n*, 56*n*, 61*n*, 65*n*

Savana Town, 61, 62, 67, 68

Saxapahaw Indians: at Keyauwee Town, 23; in *soc-ca-hick* alliance, xxviii, 23; as suspects in attack on South Carolina traders, 8*n*; and Wateree slave raiders, xxxiii–xxxiv, 9–10, 10*n*

Seed, Patricia, xxii*n*, xxiii*n*, 47*n*

Seneca Indians: and English colonists, xxiv, xxvii, xxviii*n*; mourning wars, xxiv–xxv; and Occaneechi Indians, xxvii, xxviii; political organization, xxvi. *See also* Iroquois Indians; Seneca-Siouan hostilities

Seneca-Siouan hostilities, xi–xii, xxvi–xxvii, xxxiv*n*, xxxvi, xli

Shakori Indians: at Ajusher, xxvi, xxvi*n*, 23*n*, 38*n*; and Eno Indians, 18; and Eno Will, xxvi; in *soc-ca-hick* alliance, xxxv, 23

INDEX

Shefveland, Kristalyn M., xvi*n*, xxxvi*n*
Sherman, William H., xxxvi*n*
silver project: Board of Trade, xiii, xviii, xxx, xli*n*, xlvi, xlvii, 5*n*, 57–59, 57*n*, 61–64, 62*n*, 65, 67–68; Moore's interference, 58*n*, 59*n*, 62, 62*n*, 63, 65, 66; partners in, xiii, xiv, xxx, xlvii, 59, 61*n*, 63, 65, 68; and Traunter's treks, xxx, xxxi*n*; and William III, xxxii*n*, xxxvi, xli, 57, 59, 62–63, 65, 66, 67, 68
Siouan-Iroquoian warfare. *See* Seneca-Siouan hostilities
Sirmans, M. Eugene, xxxiii*n*, 54*n*, 58*n*
slaves, Indian: captives of Indian wars, xxiv–xxv, 10, 10*n*; conditions of, xxiv–xxv, xxv*n*, xxxiii*n*; cost of, xxxii. *See also* Indian Jack; Indian slave trade; Wateree Jack
slave trade, Indian. *See* Indian slave trade
smallpox: impact of, xxv, 26*n*; and Indian slave trade, xii, xxv, xxvi; in Southeast, xii, xxv, 26*n*; at Suteree Town, xliv, 26; at Waxhaw Town, xxxix, 27. *See also* doctors, Indigenous; healing practices; sweat lodges
Smith, Capt. John; as colonial writer, xxxvi–xxxvii, xxxvii*n*; *Generall Historie of Virginia, New-England and the Summer Isles*, xxxvii; *Map of Virginia*, xxxvii; and Powhatan Indians, xxiii
Smith, John: "Abstract of the Proceedings relating to the Discovery of Silver Mines in Carolina," xlvii; "Humble Memorial of John Smith," xlvii; on Moore's interference with silver project, 62, 62*n*, 65, 65*n*, 66; politician, xiv, xvii, 61*n*; silver project partner, xiv, xiv*n*, xvii*n*, xlvii, 59, 61–64, 63*n*, 65–66; and Traunter, xvii*n*, 63, 64
soc-ca-hick (Eno Will's commission): as Anglo-Indian peace pact, xii, xxx, xxxv, 3, 23; as Anglo-Indian trade pact, xii, xxxi*n*, xxxiv, xxxv, 21, 22, 23, 38, 39; as anti-Occaneechi pact, xxxiv, xxxv, xxxvi, 21, 42; ceremony at Ajusher, xxxv, 39–40, 42; ceremony at Keyauwee Town, 23; ceremony at Occaneechi Town, xxxv, 21; and Eno Will, xii, xxxiv, xxxv, xxxv*n*, 21, 22, 23, 24, 38, 39, 40, 42, 49; as inter-Indian diplomacy, xxxv*n*, 23, 42; and Tuscarora Indians, xxxv*n*, 42; and Waxhaw village, 49

Spanish in the Southeast, xxi–xxii, 18*n*
Speck, William A., xiv*n*, xlvi*n*, 5*n*
Sprat, Thomas, xxxviii; *History of the Royal Society of London for the Improving of Natural Knowledge*, xxxviii
Spufford, Margaret, xvi*n*
Stephenson, Robert L., 30*n*, 53*n*
Stern, Jessica, xvi, xvii*n*, xxxiv*n*
Stevens (Stephens), Robert, Jr.: attack on, xxxiii, 8–9, 8*n*, 9*n*, 40–42; as Moore's trader, xxxiii, xxxiii*n*, 8; as South Carolina slave trader, xxxiii–xxxiv; and Traunter's revenge motive, xxx, xxxiii, xxxiv, 9, 10
Sugaree Indians, xx, xxxiii, 8*n*, 26*n*, 49*n*
Suteree Indians: healing practices of Suteree doctor, 26; language, 27; location of town, 26*n*; size of cornfields, xliv, 26–27; and smallpox, xii, xxv, 26, 26*n*; Traunter's route to, 36
Swanton, John R., 27*n*, 46*n*
sweat lodges, 26, 27

Tanner, Henry, 31*n*, 32*n*
Tinling, Marion, xv*n*, 9*n*
Tomahittan Indians: as Cherokees, 40*n*; as Hitchiti-speaking from Georgia, xxxiv*n*, 40*n*; in Needham and Arthur, xl, 40*n*; as from New York, xxxiv*n*, 41, 41*n*; and Occaneechi-Tomahittan attack on South Carolina traders, xxxiv, xxxiv*n*, xl, xli, xliii, 40–42
Town Creek (archaeological site), xxix, 28*n*, 44*n*, 45*n*
trade: at Appomattox store, xv, xviii–xix, xxviii, xxxiii, 9; customs for, xxii–xxiii, xxxv, xlii, xliv, 20, 20*n*, 21, 27, 39; in European goods, xxix, xxxv*n*, xliii, 20, 50, 59, 64; Indian-Indian, xxi; intercolonial competition for, xxxii, xxxvi, xli, xlii. *See also* Indian slave trade
trade pact. *See soc-ca-hick*

93

INDEX

trade paths/roads: cross roads, 25, 25*n*, 44*n*; Esaw path/Catawba path, xi*n*, 11; fords, xii, 15*n*, 24*n*, 30*n*, 37*n*, 44, 52*n*; "main" trade road, xxxi*n*, xxxii*n*, xliv, xlv, xlv*n*, 11*n*, 16*n*, 38*n*, 43*n*; mileage for, xlv, xlv*n*, 53*n*; Native meaning of, xxi; "new" road, xxvii–xxix, xxx, xxxi, xxxi*n*, xxxii*n*, xxxvi, xliii, xlv, 36, 45*n*; Occaneechi path, xi*n*, 11; Traunter's route in 1698, 11, 11*n*, 13*n*, 15*n*, 22*n*, 24*n*, 34, 36; Traunter's route in 1699, 35, 37*n*, 38, 43, 43*n*, 45*n*, 47*n*, 50, 56; Tuscarora road, 13*n*; Virginia traders' path, xi, xix, 11, 13*n*, 15*n*, 16*n*, 22*n*, 24*n*, 25*n*, 36; Waxhaw road (old trade path), xi*n*, xxxi, xxxi*n*, xliv, 11, 29*n*, 35, 47, 47*n*, 48, 49, 49*n*, 50

traders: abuses by, xxxiv, xxxvi; Byrd's, xi, xviii, xxvii*n*, xxx, xxxii, xxxiii, xxxiv, xl, xl*n*, xliii, 9, 10, 11, 11*n*, 20, 21, 23, 25, 25*n*; character of, xvi, xvii; customs of, xix, 14, 14*n*, 19, 19*n*, 47, 47*n*; as go-betweens, xxxiv; inciting Indian violence, xxxiv, xxxvi, xl, 42; and Indian women, xxi*n*, xlii, xliv; killing of, xxvii*n*, xxxiii*n*, xli, 12, 15, 40; Moore's, xxxii, xxxiii, 8, 8*n*, 40, 42; and *soc-ca-hick*, xii, xxxv, 7, 21, 22, 23, 38, 39; of South Carolina, xxxiii–xxxiv, 7*n*, 8, 8*n*, 40, 42; of Virginia, xi, xxiv, xxv, xxxii, 7*n*, 11, 23, 38, 39, 40. *See also* Couture, Jean; Hearn (Herne), John; Long, Alexander; Stevens (Stephens), Robert; Traunter, Richard

Tranter, Edward, xvii, xvii*n*, xviii, xviii*n*

Tranter's Creek (North Carolina), xvii, xvii*n*

Traunter, Richard: alliances with Indians, xii, xxviii, xxxv, xxxv*n*, 3, 23; as Byrd I's agent at Appomattox store, xi, xv, xvi, xviii, xix, xxxiii, 9, 11, 35, 63; gifting with Indians, xxix, xxxv, xlii, 20, 21, 50, 59, 64; "Humble Memorial of Edward Loughton and Richard Tranter," xlvii; Indigenous languages spoken, xi, xviii, xix, 19, 21, 42, 49, 63; mileage discrepancies, xlv–xlvi*n*, 53–54*n*; and silver project, xiii, xviii, xxx, xxxi, xxxii, xxxvi, xli, xlvi, xlvii, xlviii, 57–59, 63, 64, 66. *See also soc-ca-hick*

Trinkley, Michael, 30*n*

Troxler, Carole, 22*n*

Tucker, Norma, xxx*n*

Turkey Creek (South Carolina), 32, 32*n*, 55, 55*n*

Turner, E. Randolph, III, xx*n*, xxiii*n*, xxiv*n*

Tuscarora Indians: and Eno Indians, xxvi, 18; and Eno Will, xxviii, xxxv, 42; as Iroquois, xxvi, xxvi*n*, 18*n*; and Nottoway Indians, xxxv*n*; and Occaneechi Indians, xxxv, 42; political organization, xx; and *soc-ca-hick*, xxviii, xxxv, xxxv*n*, 42; and South Carolina slave raiders, xxix; territory, xx, xxvi, xxvi–xxviii*n*, xxviii–xxix, 18*n*; towns, xii*n*, xx, xxix; and trade, xviii, xxviii, xxxv*n*

Tuscarora language: as trade language, xi, xviii, 19, 19*n*, 21, 42; Traunter spoke, xi, xix, 19, 21

Uwharrie Mountains, xi, xxix, 35, 43*n*

Uwharrie River, 24*n*, 58*n*

Virginia Museum of History and Culture, xiii, xiii*n*, xvi*n*, xlviii

Wachob, Andrew, 30*n*

Ward, H. Trawick, xxvii, xxxv, xxxv*n*, 8*n*, 19*n*, 23*n*

Waselkov, Gregory A., xxi*n*, xxv*n*, xxxiv*n*, 40*n*

Wateree Indians: in Cofitachequi chiefdom, xx, 49*n*; food gifts to Traunter, 27; and Indian Jack, xxxiii, 9; language, 27, 49; location of, xxxi*n*, xlv*n*, 27*n*; and Moore, xxxii; as slave raiders, xxxii, xxxiii, xxxvi, 9–10, 10*n*; trade with Virginia, xix

Wateree Jack: enslaved by Moore, xv, xv*n*; as Indian Jack, xv, 8*n*

Wateree River, 29*n*, 47*n*, 50*n*

Waxhaw Indians at Waxhaw Town: afterlife, xxxix, xliii, 28, 28*n*; burial, xxxix, 27–28; in Cofitachequi chiefdom, xx; healing practices, xii, 27; language, 27;

INDEX

location of, 27*n*; mourning ritual, 28; and smallpox, xii, xxv, xxxix, 26*n*; and South Carolina, xviii; sweat lodge, 27; trade with Virginia, xix

Waxhaw Indians at Waxhaw village: in Cofitachequi chiefdom, xx, 49*n*; corn fields, 49; and Eno Will, xxviii, xxix, xliv, 49; games, 49, 49*n*; gifts given by Traunter, 50; language, 49; location of, 49*n*, 50*n*; women's refusal of hospitality for Traunter, xlii, xliv, 49

Webber, Mabel, xxxiii*n*, 54*n*

Weber, David J., xxii*n*

Westo Indians: and Indian slave trade, xxiv, xxv, xxxii; as Iroquois, xxiv; and Moore, xxxii; and South Carolina, xxv; and Virginia, xxiv, xxv

Widmer, Randolph J., xx*n*

William III (king): and silver project, xxx, xxxii*n*, xxxvi, xli, 57, 59, 61*n*, 63, 63*n*, 67, 68

Williams, David, xxxi*n*

Woccon Indians, 46, 46*n*

Wood, Abraham: Needham and Arthur narrative, xxxvii, xxxvii*n*, 40*n*; and Tomahittans, xl, 40*n*

Wood, Peter H., xvii*n*

Woodward, Henry, xxii

Wright, J. Leitch, Jr., xv, xx*n*, xxiv*n*, xxv*n*, xxix, xxx*n*, 9*n*, 49*n*

Yadkin Ford, xxvii, 24*n*, 25*n*

Yadkin River, xxviii, 24, 24*n*, 25, 25*n*, 35, 44*n*, 45, 45*n*, 46

Yuchi Indians, xxxiv, xxxiv*n*

EARLY AMERICAN HISTORIES

Making the Early Modern Metropolis: Culture and Power in Pre-Revolutionary Philadelphia
Daniel P. Johnson

The Permanent Resident: Excavations and Explorations of George Washington's Life
Philip Levy

From Independence to the U.S. Constitution: Reconsidering the Critical Period of American History
Douglas Bradburn and Christopher R. Pearl, editors

Washington's Government: Charting the Origins of the Federal Administration
Max M. Edling and Peter J. Kastor, editors

The Natural, Moral, and Political History of Jamaica, and the Territories thereon Depending, from the First Discovery of the Island by Christopher Columbus to the Year 1746
James Knight, edited by Jack P. Greene

Statute Law in Colonial Virginia: Governors, Assemblymen, and the Revisals That Forged the Old Dominion
Warren M. Billings

Against Popery: Britain, Empire, and Anti-Catholicism
Evan Haefeli, editor

Conceived in Crisis: The Revolutionary Creation of an American State
Christopher R. Pearl

Redemption from Tyranny: Herman Husband's American Revolution
Bruce E. Stewart

Experiencing Empire: Power, People, and Revolution in Early America
Patrick Griffin, editor

Citizens of Convenience: The Imperial Origins of American Nationhood on the U.S.-Canadian Border
Lawrence B. A. Hatter

"Esteemed Bookes of Lawe" and the Legal Culture of Early Virginia
Warren M. Billings and Brent Tarter, editors

Settler Jamaica in the 1750s: A Social Portrait
Jack P. Greene

Loyal Protestants and Dangerous Papists: Maryland and the Politics of Religion in the English Atlantic, 1630–1690
Antoinette Sutto

The Road to Black Ned's Forge: A Story of Race, Sex, and Trade on the Colonial American Frontier
Turk McCleskey

Dunmore's New World: The Extraordinary Life of a Royal Governor in Revolutionary America—with Jacobites, Counterfeiters, Land Schemes, Shipwrecks, Scalping, Indian Politics, Runaway Slaves, and Two Illegal Royal Weddings
James Corbett David

Creating the British Atlantic: Essays on Transplantation, Adaptation, and Continuity
Jack P. Greene

The Evil Necessity: British Naval Impressment in the Eighteenth-Century Atlantic World
Denver Brunsman

Early Modern Virginia: Reconsidering the Old Dominion
Douglas Bradburn and John C. Coombs, editors

www.ingramcontent.com/pod-product-compliance
Lightning Source LLC
Chambersburg PA
CBHW030900170426
43193CB00009BA/685